Fort Clatsop: Rebuilding an Icon

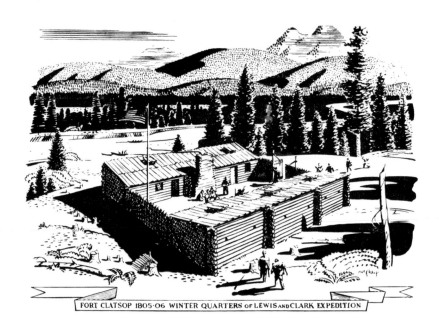

FORT CLATSOP 1805-06 WINTER QUARTERS OF LEWIS AND CLARK EXPEDITION

This depiction of the first Fort Clatsop replica was drawn by Rolf Klep, an artist living in Astoria during the 1950s when the replica was built. (Drawing from the Clatsop County Historical Society.)

Fort Clatsop: Rebuilding an Icon

The Daily Astorian

Ooligan Press
Portland, Oregon

ISBN 978-1-9-932010-18-3

Cover design by Karli Clift.
Interior design by Jennifer Omner.
Maps on page 45, 54, and 57 by Andy Freed.
Front cover photo by Alex Pajunas of *The Daily Astorian*.
Back cover photos 1–3 by Lori Assa and 4 by Sue Cody of *The Daily Astorian*.

This publication is the product of Ooligan Press and the Publishing Program of the Center for Excellence in Writing at Portland State University. It was produced by the students of this program, with mapping assistance from the Portland State University Center for Spatial Analysis and Research. For credits, see back matter.

Ooligan Press • Portland State University
P.O. Box 751 • Portland, OR 97207-0751
ooligan@pdx.edu • www.ooliganpress.pdx.edu

10 9 8 7 6 5 4 3 2 1

Printed in China.

 Portland State
UNIVERSITY

CONTENTS

FOREWORD   7
PREFACE   11

ALARM IN THE NIGHT   15
Mystery fire disrupts Lewis and Clark Bicentennial

FORT CLATSOP'S RESURRECTION   27
Community pride sparks memorial

SEARCHING FOR FORT CLATSOP   55
Historians uncover details and fresh perspectives

THE SHOW MUST GO ON   75
In the midst of rebuild, Bicentennial proceeds

REBUILDING AN ICON   99
New replica rises from the ashes

ADDITIONAL RESOURCES   125

A stake is driven to mark the Fort Clatsop site in 1900.
(Photo from the Clatsop County Historical Society.)

FOREWORD

by Rex Ziak
Fort Clatsop is the oldest American historic site west of the Rocky Mountains—and so, it should be no surprise to learn that its long, long existence has become an intriguing story. What other site in America can claim to have been built, abandoned, then lost and forgotten—only to be rediscovered and reconstructed, then tragically destroyed and constructed once again?

Fort Clatsop's story begins at the end of an extraordinary journey. In November of 1805, Lewis and Clark, along with their party, had reached the Pacific Ocean. Then, in pursuit of elk, they crossed the Columbia River, found a suitable location for a winter camp, and quickly constructed a seven-room log cabin. They named this temporary home Fort Clatsop.

What became of the little log fort immediately after Lewis and Clark's departure in March of 1806 is rather unclear. All we know for sure is that in fewer than six years from that date, curious newcomers to the area were searching for this historic site.

These "newcomers" were members of the Astor Party that arrived by ship in March of 1811. The party was determined to establish a fur trading post at the mouth of the Columbia. They worked nonstop all summer constructing a warehouse, bunkhouse, and stockade, but in early October one man slipped away from the group with the intention of visiting Fort Clatsop.

Barely five and a half years had passed since Lewis and Clark's departure when Gabriel Franchere wrote in his journal: "It was on that day at Youngs Bay, where I saw the ruins of the quarters erected by Captains Lewis and Clark in 1805–06: they were but piles of rough, unhewn logs, overgrown with parasite creepers."

In May of the following year another group from the Astor Party made a pilgrimage to the site of Fort Clatsop. Ross Cox wrote in his journal: "We also visited Fort Clatsop, the place where Captains Lewis and Clark spent the winter of 1805–06; . . . The logs of the house were still standing and marked with the names of several of the party."

In 1813, on the day immediately following the official transfer of the Columbia Territory into British possession, and with the Union Jack fluttering in the breeze above "Fort George," several British citizens searched for Lewis and Clark's campsite. Alexander Henry wrote:

> We walked up to see the old American winter quarters of Captains Lewis and Clark in 1805–06, which are in total ruins, the wood having been cut down and destroyed by the Indians; but the remains are still visible. In the fort are already grown up shoots of willows 25 feet high. The place is deeply shaded with spruce, pine, sapin, etc.; the woods seemed gloomy and dark, the beams of the sun being prevented from reaching the ground through so thick a foliage.

Exactly how many Euro-Americans visited Fort Clatsop in these early years will never be known. Did these men seek out this place merely to see where the Corps camped; or did these early explorers feel some camaraderie and respectful brotherhood with one another?

By the 1850s the era of the explorers and fur trappers had passed and the Oregon Trail was radically transforming the Pacific Northwest. Tens of thousands of immigrants flooded into Oregon. It was a new generation with new stories to tell, and, soon, the venerable "old timers" were those who had arrived in the first wagon trains. Silently and unobserved, the remains of the earliest outposts and trading houses collapsed as their log walls rotted beneath thick blankets of moss.

It is possible the loggers who felled the old-growth trees towering around Lewis and Clark's campsite might have paused for a moment and gazed at the decayed remains of old Fort Clatsop, but they would not have delayed for very long. These cutters were paid to swing an axe, and they had hungry families to feed.

The 1890s was a boom-time. Boatloads of hardworking Scandinavians, as well as immigrants from other countries, arrived—along the waterfront of Astoria a passerby would hear Finnish, Swedish, Danish, Norwegian, Italian, and Chinese spoken as often as English. Salmon canneries and logging camps were running strong. It's likely that a majority of Clatsop County residents had never heard of Lewis and Clark.

Suddenly, in August of 1899, a curious stranger arrived on a boat from Portland. He was interested in only one thing: he wanted to visit the winter campsite of Lewis and Clark. His name was Olin D. Wheeler and he was a publicist and writer for the Northern Pacific

Railway. His current assignment was to travel the entire Lewis and Clark route and then write a book. Wheeler was led to the site, and, with little hard evidence, concluded that it was the correct location. Several photographs were taken, and everyone went back home, but Wheeler had piqued the interest of the Oregon Historical Society.

In 1901, the Oregon Historical Society purchased three acres of land around the site. Several years later the first publication of Lewis and Clark's journals brought Fort Clatsop to the forefront. Everyone could now read about what had occurred, and the Astorians soon realized that it was they—not Portland, not Seaside—who had possession of a great historical site.

But it still took another 50 years before the fort would be resurrected. The 150th anniversary of the Lewis and Clark expedition brought attention to the site and stirred up an interest and pride among the local community. The citizens of Clatsop County were determined to honor the site and it was they—not the federal government, the historical society, or the state—who would establish a replica of Lewis and Clark's fort. This was their historic site and they were determined to honor it.

This book is a story about more than a replica of a historic campsite. This is a story of a community that has proudly shown, time and time again, that the location of Lewis and Clark's winter camp will be forever honored.

Rex Ziak is a local historian who made a detailed study of Lewis and Clark's time in the Lower Columbia River. His research revealed the true western end of their journey and redefined their entire history in the region, which helped lead to the creation of a new national park.

PREFACE

When the phone rings in the middle of the night, it's trouble. Lewis and Clark National Historical Park Superintendent Chip Jenkins got that call the night Fort Clatsop burned. So did *The Daily Astorian's* reporter Tom Bennett.

It is said that newspapers write the first draft of history. Bennett accomplished that much in the ensuing days. With a pen and reporter's notebook in hand, Bennett foraged for the story behind the fort's immolation. Even as *The Daily Astorian* staff scurried to meet deadlines and deliver the news, the editors realized they had a much larger story to report.

In the communities near the mouth of the Columbia River, there is genuine affection for the National Park Service and deep respect for Fort Clatsop and the Lewis and Clark story. The emotional response to the fort's burning was akin to learning that a sudden calamity had visited your neighbor. For *The Daily Astorian*, this was an emotional and local story with deep roots in American history.

Thus, Tom Bennett was commissioned to reach far beyond the breaking news and explore the history and archaeology of the Fort Clatsop replica and historic site. Bennett's enthusiasm for the history beat showed in the energy and color he brought to the Fort Clatsop story.

In this book, *The Daily Astorian* used Bennett's stories and additional research to create a second draft of history. *Fort Clatsop: Rebuilding an Icon* is *The Daily Astorian*'s tribute to the spirit of the community that has built two replicas. Most of all it is a testament to the power of an icon.

Stephen A. Forrester
Editor & Publisher
The Daily Astorian

The fort burns. (Photo courtesy of Lewis and Clark National Historical Park, National Park Service.)

Alarm in the Night

Mystery fire disrupts
Lewis and Clark Bicentennial

ASTORIA, Oregon—Late at night on October 3, 2005, an Astoria resident gazed across the bay and saw flames shooting up through the fog and rain. It was ten minutes after ten when the woman picked up the phone. She wanted those in charge to see what she saw.

> *Caller:* "I see a fire, I'm sure it's already been reported, but I live on Sonora, on the hill in Astoria, I'm looking over Youngs Bay River . . ."
>
> *9-1-1 Dispatcher:* "Yeah, it's kind of foggy and raining out. Sometimes that happens . . ."
>
> *Caller:* " . . . okay . . ."
>
> *9-1-1 Dispatcher:* " . . . yeah, it's not a fire."
>
> *Caller:* "Really? It looks like a fire on the other side of the river."
>
> *9-1-1 Dispatcher:* "Yeah, it's not a fire."

Ten minutes later, the Communication Center for Astoria Regional Dispatch received another call from near Captain Robert Gray Elementary School. Luckily, the second caller reached a different dispatcher. The caller asked if a controlled burn was scheduled somewhere across the river. She couldn't pinpoint the exact location of the fire, but she said she believed she saw bright orange flaring near Airport Road.

"There's a lot of smoke with it," the woman said.

"Okay, we'll have someone check it out," the second dispatcher told her.

Lewis and Clark Fire Chief Ian O'Connor told the dispatcher to alert department volunteers to the south end of The Old Youngs Bay Bridge, and at 10:28 p.m. the dispatcher sounded the official alarm.

Firefighters from Lewis and Clark, Olney-Walluski, Astoria, and Warrenton departments mop up the ruins of Fort Clatsop. (Photo by Lori Assa, The Daily Astorian.)

The siren came too late. By the time the first firefighters arrived at Fort Clatsop, flames had engulfed the county's most cherished landmark. The delay likely cost the department about 15 minutes—that wouldn't have been enough time to save the fort, but it might have allowed firefighters to protect some of the structure, O'Connor said.

About 30 firefighters from the Lewis and Clark, Olney-Walluski, Astoria, and Warrenton fire departments fought the blaze for a little over an hour, but the flames already had destroyed one side of the log fort and gutted the other.

By the time firefighters hosed out the last flames, virtually every

The side of the fort containing the men's quarters (left) suffered the most damage, though the captains' quarters are also charred and gutted. (Photo by Lori Assa, The Daily Astorian.)

piece of wood in the 50-square-foot replica had been touched by the fire. The flames would have spread quickly and burned especially hot in the log structure, O'Connor said.

Scott Stonum, the park's chief of resources, watched firefighters hose down the remaining hot spots among the ruins. "I'm still wondering if I'm awake," he said.

The destruction of the beloved monument stunned the entire community. The following day, supporters of Fort Clatsop converged on the park to view the damage and offer condolences to one another.

The gate to Fort Clatsop was one of the few pieces of wood untouched by the fire. (Photo courtesy of The Daily Astorian.)

"It makes me heartsick," said Michael Foster, who served as the fort's first guide in the 1950s and was the head of the Fort Clatsop Historical Association in 2005. "People worked so hard for so many years to make this a place they could be proud of."

"A lot of people from the community put their hearts into this and supported Fort Clatsop," Stonum said. "It's a part of the community. I feel for that."

Cyndi Mudge, executive director of "Destination: The Pacific," the Lewis and Clark Bicentennial event, set to take place six weeks after the fire, viewed the ruins in amazement.

"Our office is right here, and I have the opportunity to see people come in, the kids seeing it for the first time, parents who came here when they were kids. Fort Clatsop has a lot of memories for a lot of people in the whole state."

In 1955, community volunteers built the first replica of the Lewis and Clark Expedition's winter quarters of 1805–1806. Renovations throughout the decades had increased the historical accuracy of the structure, and the building was the focal point of Lewis and Clark National Historical Park. It was to be the center of the North Coast's role in the national Lewis and Clark Bicentennial Commemoration that would take place on November 11–15, 2005.

Even on the day after the fire, the visitors' center remained open to the public. The park welcomed an Elderhostel group who arrived at the end of an 18-day journey along the entire Lewis and Clark Trail. Each year, about 9,000 school children attended the park's various education programs, and as many as 70 kids a day visited Fort Clatsop, taking part in activities at the fort and at the visitors' center. The park was a much-anticipated part of the local fourth-grade Oregon history section, so the day after the fire, employees at Fort Clatsop welcomed a group of students from Lewis and Clark Elementary School with some improvised activities for the "Class of Discovery" program.

The afternoon before the fire, a group of schoolchildren attended one of the fort's interpretive programs and warmed themselves over the fire that most likely caused the fort's demise.

Park Superintendent Chip Jenkins said that fires were lit in two of the fort's fireplaces on that Monday afternoon—just after a countywide burn ban, in effect since August, had been lifted. Fires were frequently lit to add to the frontier-life feel for visitors, but in dry summer months, fires were restricted. Three years ago, sections of the fort were scorched due to a fire in one of the fireplaces. In response, all fireplaces and chimneys were rebuilt to protect the surrounding wood structure. The park staff also created protocols to ensure that fires remained small, were burned for only a limited period, and were thoroughly extinguished before the fort closed.

But on October 3rd, those protocols and safeguards failed. Three weeks after the fire, investigators from the federal Bureau of Alcohol, Tobacco, Firearms and Explosives (ATF)—assisted by state authorities, local police, and fire agencies—and the National Park Service linked the initial sparks to the open-pit fireplace in the enlisted men's quarters.

John McMahon, ATF special agent, said interviews with park staff revealed that burning embers occasionally floated out from the open hearth and landed on the floor, where they were ground out by park staff. It is possible that an ember flew out and wasn't noticed, given the smoky conditions that were normal in the rooms when fires were lit. The investigation also revealed that the room's rough-cut, cedar-plank floor contained dry rot, which would have made the wood more susceptible to fire.

Along with the ATF, the investigators included personnel from the Oregon State Police, the Oregon State Fire Marshal, and the local fire departments, as well as a specially trained search dog.

The investigators "meticulously (went) through the entire scene," but found no evidence of gasoline or other accelerants or such fuels as wadded-up newspaper, McMahon said. On the night of the fire, a

An investigator inspects the damage done by the October 3rd fire.
(Photo courtesy of The Daily Astorian.)

slight suspicion of arson was raised when Fire Chief O'Connor, the first man on the scene, saw a dark Chevy pick-up truck leaving the park long after employees would have left the premises. Investigators attempted to locate the truck but abandoned the lead when evidence pointed away from arson.

"There is no conclusive evidence that the fire was intentionally set," McMahon concluded.

The day after the fire, as the ruins continued to smolder, an exhausted and somewhat tearful Chip Jenkins said a new Fort Clatsop would rise from the ashes to replace the building erected 50 years ago.

"The rebuilding process is starting today," Jenkins exclaimed before he met with community leaders to begin sketching out a plan for the project.

Park Superintendent Chip Jenkins gives an interview after the fire. (Photo courtesy of The Daily Astorian.)

But would it be ready in time for the bicentennial of Lewis and Clark? With the commemoration just six weeks away, park employees and community members began the rebuilding process with their eyes on commemorating the past for future generations.

"Yes, we will rebuild," Jenkins said. "Just like the absolutely fabulous people in the community who built the replica."

The fire reduced most of the fort to charred logs.
(Photo courtesy of Lewis and Clark National Historical Park, National Park Service.)

Fort "Fix-it Man" Helps Douse the Flames

Ron Tyson responded to the Fort Clatsop fire as chief of the Olney-Walluski Fire and Rescue District, but he knew the park from his 23 years as the maintenance supervisor.

"Other than the original builders, no one's got more in that fort than I do," he said.

"You see that chimney?" he said to firefighters and seasonal park ranger Sean Johnson, as they mopped up the fire. "I helped build it."

When he first arrived at the fort, Ron Tyson was shocked to see the historic fort in flames.

"That's the last thing I expected or wanted to see," he said.

As an employee of the park, Tyson was distraught watching the fifty-year-old replica of Lewis and Clark's winter encampment destroyed. But as chief of the Olney-Walluski Fire and Rescue District, he also had a job to do. After taking a moment or two to get over his shock, he got to work helping to coordinate the efforts of the four fire departments that responded to the blaze.

Tyson probably had more intimate knowledge of the fort replica than anyone else. It was his job to keep the historic structure in good repair, protecting it against the effects of time, weather, and hundreds of thousands of visitors.

"Just making sure the place was functioning" was how Tyson described his job as the fort's maintenance supervisor.

Looking for work in the recession of the early 1980s, Tyson

applied for and got a job at Fort Clatsop, where he was responsible for upkeep of all the facilities.

The fort replica, built by community volunteers in 1955, was very well put together, Tyson said, but the damp climate inevitably took its toll on some parts of the structure. One of his first major projects at the fort was splitting some cedar logs to replace the rotting floor. The maintenance crew also replaced some of the logs near the ground, a job that required them to raise the entire building on jacks.

There also were regular repairs and maintenance to doors, furniture, and other fixtures.

"When you have 10,000 school kids a year come through, they like to swing on the doors," Tyson will tell you. "Our mission was to make it look like we didn't do it," he said.

But as repairs were made, the park took advantage of new research to make changes for the sake of historical accuracy. In 2001, when the roof was replaced, Tyson and his crew put in longer boards, replacing the small shakes installed in the 1980s.

Prior to the fire, the machine-cut pickets—dubbed "pencils" because of their overly clean, sharp appearance—were replaced with more authentic-looking hand-peeled and hand-cut logs.

During summers, Tyson splits his time between Fort Clatsop and his other job as a professional wilderness firefighter, a career he began in 1971 digging fire lines. Eventually he worked his way up the ranks, operating as chief for an interagency group that fights wildfires all over the Western United States.

Burnby Bell, Gene Hallaux, Marvin Reed, and Otto Owen (from left) break ground for the first replica at the fort site in 1955. (Photo courtesy of Lewis and Clark National Historical Park, National Park Service.)

Fort Clatsop's Resurrection

The fledgling Junior Chamber of Commerce (Jaycees) members were thinking more along the lines of a clubhouse, not a national park, when they hit on the idea of building a replica of Lewis and Clark's Fort Clatsop in the early 1950s.

"We were young enough, we didn't know it couldn't be done," said Chuck Lauderdale, who helped found the Jaycees club in 1953.

A critical editorial printed in *The Oregonian* in October 1953, and reprinted in the *Astoria Budget*, sparked the group's interest in the park. The editorial bemoaned the weeds and litter that cluttered the old fort site, which at that time was marked only with a plaque and a flagpole.

The Jaycees club was a new service group, open to young men 21 to 35 years old.

The original plan was simply to clean up and restore the overgrown, trash-strewn park. They pulled out blackberry vines, repainted restrooms, and restored the bronze marker. Wes Shaner and Wilt Paulson first came up with the idea of building a fort replica for the

150th anniversary celebration of Lewis and Clark's arrival at the Pacific Ocean in August 1955, according to a Bob Lovell, a member of the original group.

Shaner was one of the driving forces behind the project. According to Ruth Shaner, Wes Shaner's wife, the Jaycees were looking for a civic project that would leave "a lasting contribution" to the community, and they focused on the neglected Fort Clatsop site. "They wanted to prove what they could accomplish," Ruth said.

Johann Mehlum, Wilt Paulson, and Jon Nerenberg (from left) help assemble the first replica at the fort site. (Photo courtesy of Lewis and Clark National Historical Park, National Park Service.)

"We had no idea it would be such a big deal," Chuck Lauderdale said. "It was just going to be a local clubhouse: look what it turned into."

The Jaycees had a far-fetched idea and lots of enthusiasm but no money or fort-building skills. It would take the entire community to turn the trash-strewn lot into the log structure that became the centerpiece of the Lewis and Clark National Historical Park.

The group immediately started gathering support. Shaner was named project manager and Clatsop County Historical Society member Burnby Bell was named to assist him. Astoria artist Rolf Klep researched the fort and drew plans for the replica. Copies of his sketches were sold for $10 each to raise money for the rebuild.

"I don't know where you would find a community where kids would find this kind of support," said Lovell, president of the local Chamber of Commerce. "It was just a project that appealed to everybody."

Crown Zellerbach Corporation, a lumber company, not only donated 408 logs but also paid to have them treated. "If we're going to build the thing, let's make it last 50 years," Ed Stamm, Crown Zellerbach's vice president, was quoted as saying.

Other people came forward to offer money, labor, and supplies. The $40,000 raised was almost entirely from small contributions, but no local, state, or federal funds were provided for the construction of the replica.

The Jaycees approached the Lions, "the only club in town with money," who agreed to build the foundation for the structure. The Clatsop County Historical Society was also a key player in the project. Bell was "a real sparkplug" who lent his efforts to the fundraising campaign, Lovell said.

The organizers even received some unsolicited help in pinpointing the project site. An elderly Seaside resident, who grew up in the area and played in the old fort as a child, walked the grounds with Wes Shaner, pointing out landmarks he remembered from his youth. "He convinced Wes that this was the site," Ruth Shaner said.

When the number of volunteers dwindled and the work slowed, Ruth hit on the idea of offering activities for kids at the work site, which brought out several moms and dads whose labor put the project back on track.

Jaycees's President Wilt Paulson, also the local airport manager, arranged to have the fort assembled in the airport's hangar. Once built, the replica's logs were numbered for identification. The entire structure was then disassembled and sent to the Wauna Mill where the logs were wolmanized, a preservation technique recommended by Crown Zellerbach. Much to the community's dismay, this process removed all the reassembly marks. The fort had to be rebuilt in the hangar, marked, and disassembled for a second time before it could be moved to the site. There it was reassembled for the third and final time.

The Finnish Brotherhood of Astoria supplied skilled carpenters and, under the guidance of foreman Olavi Hietaharju, who had log cabin construction experience, they built the fort using Scandinavian techniques.

Valio Rautio remembered overseeing the Jaycees "city boys" who had enthusiasm but few practical woodworking skills. Rautio and his fellow Finnish carpenters used special rounded chisels to carve out the notches where the logs would join, a skill that most local "two-by-four carpenters" didn't have. "It was not a complicated job, but it takes experience," Rautio said.

The first replica was constructed following descriptions in Clark's journals, though aided by speculation and some alterations. For example, while the journal included fireplaces, the replica was built without them. They were added in the early 1960s and continually reworked over the years.

The gates of the replica faced northeast and southwest. It was 50 feet square with seven rooms and an open space in the middle. On

Logs for the first replica undergo a preservation technique called wolmanization before being assembled. (Photo courtesy of Lewis and Clark National Historical Park, National Park Service.)

the west side of the fort were three rooms. The two outside rooms were furnished with tables and chairs and four pairs of bunk beds; the middle room had four pairs of bunks and also contained the stump of a Sitka spruce tree, smoothed off and used as a table. All the rooms contained open fire pits that were lined with a cement and clay mixture and placed at the back of the west wall. The smoke from these pits was funneled by chimneys, made from cedar planking that came a quarter of the way down the wall.

Olavi Heitaharju (left) and Wes Shaner review the fort plans.
(Photo courtesy of Lewis and Clark National Historical Park, National Park Service.)

The east side of the fort was composed of four rooms. The room closest to the southwest gate was 10 feet by 15 feet and contained a large double bed, a table, and a fire pit similar to the pits on the west side of the fort. The next room was 15 feet by 16 feet and accessible only through the two adjacent rooms. In it were two single beds, a table and chairs, and two writing desks that doubled as storage bins. This represented the captains' quarters, and was the only room that could, with some certainty, have its historical occupants identified. The room on the north side was 14 feet by 15 feet. It contained two pairs of bunks, a table and benches, and a fire pit similar to those on the west side of the fort.

The last room on the east side had no parade ground outlet, being reached through a "Dutch door" from the adjacent room. It was 10 feet by 15 feet. There was no flooring in this room and no fire pit. This room was believed to be the storeroom and had firewood, tools, and sometimes "jerked" meat stored in it.

The roof and walls of the original replica were covered with three layers of alternating cedar shakes. The roof itself sloped inward, toward the central parade ground. To increase visitor comfort, historically inaccurate gutters were added over the doors and wood chips were spread on the parade ground and trails. The southwest and northeast sides of the fort were enclosed in pickets. The southwest side had a large double gate, and the northeast side had a single gate. The walls of the replica contained gun ports, and there were no doors on the doorways leading into the parade ground.

Inside the fort, split puncheon cedar and spruce boards made the floorboards. All the doorways had raised sills to keep water out. Windows were present in all the rooms except the storage room.

When the community built the replica, the Oregon Historical Society (OHS) owned the land. While the OHS didn't interfere, it viewed the project with some skepticism. The society had been trying to establish a memorial on the land for 50 years.

SECURING THE SITE

In 1899, Olin D. Wheeler, a representative of OHS and writer for Northern Pacific Railway, and a group of interested parties visited the site in hopes of establishing the approximate location of Fort Clatsop. The group included Silas Smith, grandson of Clatsop Chief Coboway who reclaimed the land after Lewis and Clark's departure; four local residents; and a photographer. Wheeler instigated the trip because he wanted to retrace the footsteps of Lewis and Clark using information local residents had given him about the site.

In 1900, OHS decided to purchase the site, hoping to determine the exact location of the fort. Smith, local landowner Preston Gillette, and two members of the OHS returned to the site to confirm the location. They staked what they believed was the southwest corner of the fort and then placed stakes where they estimated the other corners would have been. No surveyors accompanied the group on either of these trips, and the location was based solely on the testimonies of local residents like Carlos Shane, who lived at the site during the early 1850s. Shane believed that he had seen the actual ruins of the fort and had subsequently burned some of the remaining logs. He was originally able to identify the site because of the second-growth timber surrounded by original first-growth timber. He used the topography of the land and some familiar trees to identify the site for the OHS representatives.

The Oregon Historical Society planned to build "an imposing and enduring monument to this great achievement in our national history and to the memory of the brave men who accomplished it." Completion of the monument was set for 1905, to coincide with the opening of the Northwest Industrial Exposition, later renamed the Lewis and Clark Exposition. The Exposition took place, but for

With the help of Oregon Historical Society members and local residents, Olin D. Wheeler, a writer from the Northern Pacific Railway, establish the approximate location of the fort in 1899. (Photo from the Oregon Historical Society Research Library, OrHi 1694.)

unknown reasons the monument was not built. However, OHS did purchase a three-acre tract of the Fort Clatsop site in March 1902 for $250.

In 1906 the Oregon Development League of Astoria and the OHS sought legislation for a congressional appropriation to purchase 160 acres at the site and erect a suitable monument commemorating the

Oregon Historical Society members explore the future fort replica site in 1899-1900.
(Photo from the Oregon Historical Society Research Library, OrHi 1692 & 1693.)

Lewis and Clark Expedition. Oregon Senator Charles Fulton introduced a bill asking the U.S. government to formally recognize the site. Fulton requested $10,000, but the bill died in committee.

When the OHS returned to Fort Clatsop in 1912, they could not find the original stakes they had placed years earlier, perhaps because of rapid overgrowth. They placed a bronze marker on the site, but it was later stolen.

The 1916 Organic Act created the National Park Service (NPS) and set the stage for work on a monument to Lewis and Clark. Twelve years later the OHS purchased two acres south of the site that included a spring allegedly used by Lewis and Clark. Volunteers cleared the fort site of brush and erected a flagpole with an embedded bronze plaque. Over the years, this plaque was stolen several times. It was finally removed and placed in the Oregon Historical Society collection during World War II, where it remained until the replica was built.

Progress on the monument slowed, but by 1935 NPS and the Oregon State Parks Board determined that Fort Clatsop should be managed by the state of Oregon. The Historic Site Act was signed, mandating that NPS provide preservation, interpretation, and access to American historic sites and antiquities, but NPS and the park's board agreed that day-to-day management should fall to the Oregon Historical Society. Local citizens were still dissatisfied. In 1948, the Clatsop County Historical Society tried unsuccessfully to earn national recognition for the site for the second time.

During this time, Louis Caywood, an archaeologist, was busy excavating the site for NPS. He found what he believed were five fire pits, and remnants of bones, charcoal, and two wood fragments. His findings were sent to Western Region Archaeologist Paul Schumaker, who later also excavated the site. Archaeologists determined that at least one so-called "fire pit" was actually the remains of a burned stump. The objects Caywood found were not carbon-dated and their whereabouts are now unknown. But this scant evidence convinced Caywood that he had found the original Fort Clatsop location, and people began planning to build a replica. A Hollywood studio expressed interest in using the replica for a movie, absorbing the cost to build it. Those plans fell through.

Park Debates

When the community decided to build the fort in 1953, there was considerable debate among Oregon Historical Society members about the future of the new park. Some argued that it should be turned over to the National Park Service, while others were reluctant to give up what they saw as the community's treasure.

The core organizers of the project chose their side in the debate early on. "It was in the back of Wes's mind from the beginning that the replica could become a national park," Wes Shaner's wife said.

Thomas Vaughan, the Oregon Historical Society's director, agreed with Shaner. Vaughan felt that if the site was to reach its full potential, it needed to be in the hands of the federal government. The society, with its limited resources, could not provide that future.

Franklin Queen, a Portland physician, wrote a letter to Douglas McKay, the Secretary of the Interior in 1955 and a former Oregon governor, and to Oregon Congressman A. Walter Norblad calling for national recognition of the fort. Meanwhile, the Oregon Historical Society contacted Oregon Senator Richard L. Neuberger to enlist his aid in transferring the fort to the federal government.

Still, the group barely completed construction in time for the commemoration event. Workers hung the gates on the morning of August 21, 1955. In the afternoon, thousands of spectators looked on while several national, state, and local leaders dedicated the structure. Dignitaries on hand included Secretary of the Interior

Community members gather to commemorate the first fort replica in 1955. (Photo from the Clatsop County Historical Society.)

*A crowd watches the 1955 Fort Clatsop replica commemoration.
(Photo from the Clatsop County Historical Society.)*

Douglas McKay, Oregon Governor Paul Patterson, Washington Governor Arthur Langlie, and the presidents of the Astoria Chamber of Commerce and Astoria Junior Chamber of Commerce. Oregon Historical Society President Burt Brown Barker and Director Thomas Vaughan also participated in the ceremony.

The debate over federal versus state control continued, with vocal proponents on both sides. Some felt that the less the federal government was involved, the better it would be for the state. At the same time, OHS was struggling under the pressure of trying to manage the site. Editorials in *The Oregonian* and in Astoria newspapers suggested that if the state of Oregon had created a state park at the site, it would not have been necessary to turn to the federal government for its protection. Senator Neuberger, who would be responsible for drafting the enabling legislation for the memorial, wrote in newspaper editorials in 1956 that it was disturbing how much criticism he received from "people who make a fetish of opposing anything associated with the national government."

Clatsop County residents who helped construct the fort joined the lobbying efforts. At the urging of Senator Neuberger, Ruth Shaner sent out Lewis and Clark medals to members of Congress to help urge them to make Fort Clatsop part of the National Park System.

Public Law 590 was signed on June 18, 1956, requiring the Department of the Interior to study the feasibility of acquiring Fort Clatsop and establishing a national memorial. National Park Service historian John A. Hussey and archaeologist Paul Schumaker were assigned to determine the viability of the project.

On May 29, 1958, President Dwight D. Eisenhower signed into law the Fort Clatsop Bill, establishing the Fort Clatsop National

Memorial "for the purpose of commemorating the culmination and the winter encampment, of the Lewis and Clark Expedition following its successful crossing of the North American continent."

In Hussey's report to the Park Service, he stated that he did not believe the replica was built on the original site but concluded that the replica was close enough. He based his conclusion on careful study of settlers' testimony, the expedition journals, and a study of the topography. Hussey recommended that surrounding land be purchased to include other possible sites for the fort and that the NPS should recognize a need for a commemoration of the Corps of Discovery. He suggested that a memorial be erected at Fort Clatsop or at one of the other Lewis and Clark sites. If Fort Clatsop were designated, he recommended that a certain minimum boundary be established to include possible sites that might have been the original site.

FINE CRAFTMANSHIP

What is almost certain is that the 1955 replica was a far more expertly crafted building than the original, which the expedition members threw together in a matter of weeks using only axes—they probably didn't even peel the bark off the logs before putting them in place. While the original fort fell into decay just a few years after the explorers' departure, the replica stood up to the elements and several improvement projects.

The builders' fine workmanship, in fact, was something of a concern to National Park Service officials when the agency took over the park and fort with the establishment of the Fort Clatsop National Memorial in 1959. Clatsop County Historical Society Curator Liisa Penner said, "The fort did not look like it was built by people just anxious to get a roof over their heads."

In the 1950s, the accuracy and legitimacy of replicas was an ongoing concern for the NPS because the organization had already made significant errors on the George Washington and Abraham Lincoln birthplace memorials. In 1959, a Historical Structures Report was done on the fort, uncovering several glaring inaccuracies. In order to use the replica as a historic exhibit it was determined that:

- Inaccurate elements such as gun ports had to be removed, and missing features, including a sentry box and windows onto the parade ground, needed to be added.
- Lewis and Clark almost certainly did not peel the logs used in construction and did little shaping of them. There was no conclusive evidence of the type of corner notch used, but based on research at Fort Mandan, another structure built by the Corps of Discovery, it was deduced that the Scandinavian method was not used.
- Chinking and daubing, which had not been done on the replica, had been done on the original.
- The wolmanized logs would need to be stained to replicate the natural weathered look.
- The roof and floor needed to be replaced with hand-hewn planking.
- A fireplace needed to be added in the captains' quarters and the rooms with fire pits required smoke vents.
- The captains' rooms, and two of the enlisted men's rooms, required half-lofts for storage.
- A water gate was needed on the opposite end of the parade ground, and all doorways required doors.

Tearing down the replica was the only way to eliminate all the glaring errors. Because of the time and money given by local residents to build the first replica, it was suggested that "the mark of the American backwoods craftsman" be used to give the fort enough authenticity for good interpretive uses. A sum of $17,000 was allocated for the changes and another $5,800 for historically accurate furnishings.

Over the next several decades, improvements to the site included a visitors' center, employee housing, and a superintendent's residence. Paul Schumaker conducted several excavations but found little evidence to indicate Lewis and Clark's presence. This may be because

The United States flag rises at the first Fort Clatsop replica. (Photo from the Clatsop County Historical Society.)

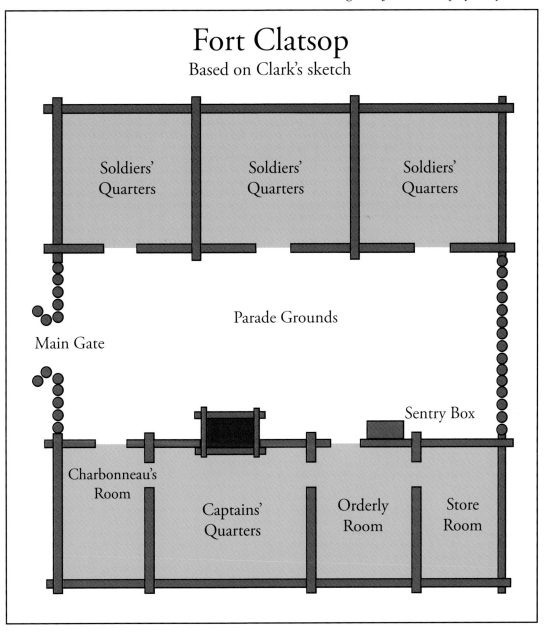

Fort Clatsop
Based on Clark's sketch

Soldiers' Quarters

Soldiers' Quarters

Soldiers' Quarters

Parade Grounds

Main Gate

Sentry Box

Charbonneau's Room

Captains' Quarters

Orderly Room

Store Room

the expedition took great care to leave the site as undisturbed as possible, or because they were running low on provisions and needed everything for the homeward trek. Another possibility is that John A. Hussey's conclusion was correct and this was not the accurate location of the original fort.

The uncertainty of the fort's original location continued to plague Fort Clatsop community members as they planned to rebuild the fort replica after the 2005 fire. It's certain that the Lewis and Clark Expedition spent the winter of 1805–1806 in the vicinity of the current park's site, but the exact location of the fort will most likely remain a mystery only Lewis and Clark could solve.

WRITER SENATOR CHAMPIONS FORT CLATSOP

When Senator Richard L. Neuberger died, *The New York Times* wrote, "Perhaps one thing on which political friends and foes of Senator Neuberger were able to agree was that he could not be ignored. One was either strongly on his side or as vehemently against him." As both a journalist and a legislator, Neuberger always took a position on controversial subjects.

Neuberger's writing career began at the University of Oregon in the 1930s, when he was the first underclassman to be elected editor of *The Oregon Daily Emerald*. He quickly turned the paper into a forum for controversial campus issues by writing editorials against fraternities, restrictions on smoking, mandatory participation in the Reserve Officer Training Corps, and compulsory student fees. Although he attended the University of Oregon as both an undergraduate and a law student, Neuberger never received a degree.

"The New Germany," published in *The Nation* in 1933, followed Neuberger's trip to Europe with his uncle Julius. It became the first exposé of Nazi tyranny over the Jews to appear in an American periodical. In the following year, as a college senior, he had his first byline in *The New York Times*. He went on to write for national publications including *Harper's*, *The Saturday Evening Post*, *Life*, *Collier's*, and *Reader's Digest*. Over the next three decades he published hundreds of articles and six books, including *The Lewis and Clark Expedition*, a children's book. He was one of the most prolific writers of his era.

Neuberger was elected to the Oregon House of Representatives shortly before the United States entered World War II. He left public service to enlist. Following a stint in the Army, he married Maurine Brown. He ran for the legislature again and was elected, this time to the Oregon Senate. Two years later, Neuberger's wife, Maurine, was elected to his former seat in the Oregon House of Representatives.

In 1954, Neuberger won a seat in the United States Senate, where he advocated for environmental protection laws, civil rights, increased funding for cancer research, the ability of voters to recall senators from office, conflict-of-interest laws, and Alaska statehood. The next year he introduced legislation requiring the Secretary of the Interior to investigate the feasibility of establishing Fort Clatsop as a national memorial. He was aware that national monuments generally have distinguishing natural resources such as the Grand Canyon or are historically significant in their own right. Memorials are meant to commemorate a person or an event, and Neuberger felt that this was a more appropriate designation for Fort Clatsop. His legislation passed the Senate with no objections.

Following Senator Neuberger's untimely death from a cerebral hemorrhage at 47, Maurine Neuberger succeeded her husband and later won re-election to his Senate seat, becoming the first Oregon woman—and only the third woman ever—to win a United States Senate election.

Richard L. Neuberger reads The Lewis & Clark Expedition, the children's book he wrote about Lewis and Clark's journey. (Photo from the Oregon Historical Society Research Library, OrHi 102850, 57500, 11015.)

Builders, History Buffs Remember Impossible Dream

Fifty years after volunteers built the Fort Clatsop replica, history buffs, as well as many of the original builders and organizers, met to reminisce about the 1955 project. Sponsored by the Clatsop County Historical Society and the National Park Service, three gatherings held in 2004 and 2005 gave the society a chance to record the history that had rested only in memories.

Society members shared newspaper photos, clippings, and flyers to spark memories and gather information about the artifacts. Many of the people and places in the photos were unidentified. In one old photograph, two men stand on top of a half-assembled log structure inside a massive building. The men appear too tiny to see in the immense space, but Valio Rautio attended the history reunions and could identify them easily—he was one of them.

"It's wonderful to put all this out there," said Bob Lovell, who shared some of his memories as one of the people involved in the original building of Fort Clatsop.

First-hand knowledge from people like Lovell and Rautio was invaluable, said Deborah Wood, cultural resource manager at the Fort Clatsop National Memorial.

While historians documented the fort's construction and inauguration at the anniversary event, there was scant information on many of the old photos, and filling in the blanks years after the fact can be difficult.

"When this was done, everyone knew everybody else, so nobody wrote anything down," Wood said.

The gatherings provided a chance to honor those who worked on the replica. Fort Clatsop Park Superintendent Chip Jenkins addressed a crowd of 30 at one of the reunions. He called it a "true, true honor" to speak to the "parents of Fort Clatsop."

"Thank you for creating a jewel of a park," he said.

Park Ranger Kyle Broberg talks to William Wagner and Ruben Solonsky (from left) at one of the three Fort Clatsop memory gatherings held at the park in 2004 and 2005. Wagner and Solonsky traveled from Eugene to attend the event. (Photo by Lori Assa, The Daily Astorian.)

Fifty years after volunteers built the Fort Clatsop replica many of the original builders and organizers met to reminisce about the 1955 project. (Photo by Lori Assa, The Daily Astorian.)

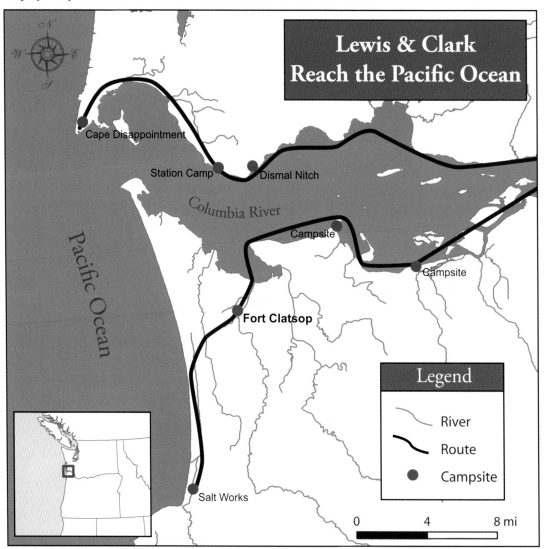

Map by Andy Freed.

Lewis & Clark
Reach the Pacific Ocean

Cape Disappointment

Station Camp   Dismal Nitch

Columbia River

Campsite

Campsite

Pacific Ocean

Fort Clatsop

Legend

～～ River

━━ Route

● Campsite

Salt Works

0   4   8 mi

Searching for Fort Clatsop

Historians uncover details and fresh perspectives
Lewis and Clark's departure from Fort Clatsop is the subject of some controversy. The official story is that the explorers gave the fort to Clatsop Chief Coboway. Tribal elders say it's not that simple.

According to Clatsop tribal history, when Lewis and Clark ended their winter at Fort Clatsop on March 23, 1806, they were riding in a stolen canoe. Lewis and Clark felt guilty and gave Fort Clatsop to Coboway.

Lewis and Clark's journals state that Chief Coboway and three members of the Clatsop tribe visited the fort on the expedition's last day. The journals assert that the captains decided to give Coboway their "houses and furniture," saying, "he has been much more kind and hospitable to us than any other Indian in this neighbourhood."

This assertion has raised controversy among tribal members. According to the Clatsop-Nehalem tribal history, Lewis and Clark didn't originally offer Fort Clatsop to the chief. At first, Lewis asked Coboway for a dugout canoe in exchange for some fishhooks and peace medals, an offer that the chief rejected.

Canoes "have a special significance to the Clatsop people," tribal councilwoman Roberta Basch said. "It's not just a boat. It comes from the trees. It has a spirit. The canoe is our life. Plus, making a dugout canoe is very time- and labor-intensive."

The chief spent ten to fifteen hunting seasons at the fort after the Corps of Discovery left, according to his grandson, Silas Smith. The fort was not suitable for regular habitation because the Clatsop people lived in one-room longhouses that lay partially underground. The fort was a multi-room structure above the ground, open to the weather and possible enemies, and it required more than one fire.

The second reason the Clatsop-Nehalem tribe disputes official history is rooted in the land itself. "Part of the problem was that this was Clatsop land," said Diane Collier, chairwoman of the Clatsop-Nehalem Tribal Council. "The Corps built a structure on our land, then gave it to the people they took the land from."

The Clatsop and Nehalem, though separate tribes during Lewis and Clark's time, have always been close culturally, socially, and politically. They shared harvesting grounds; gathered twice a year to socialize, participate in ceremonies, and partner on trades with other people; and incorporated vocabulary from one language into the other.

As one Clatsop-Nehalem history states, "When Lewis and Clark visited our territories, in the winter of 1805–1806, the Clatsop and Nehalem people were inseparable and often indistinguishable. The journals of Lewis and Clark make frequent reference to the presence of Nehalem-Tillamooks in Clatsop villages and Clatsops in Nehalem-Tillamook villages." As the white population along the northern Oregon coast grew, and the Clatsop and Nehalem were forcibly removed from their lands, the two tribes integrated even more.

Now the Clatsop-Nehalem people are of combined Clatsop and Nehalem-Tillamook ancestry, descendants of the integrated populations encountered by Lewis and Clark.

NEW BEGINNINGS

The rebuilding of Fort Clatsop and the Bicentennial offered the community and historians a chance to re-examine the details of Lewis and Clark's historic arrival at the Pacific. The fresh look at

Map by Andy Freed.

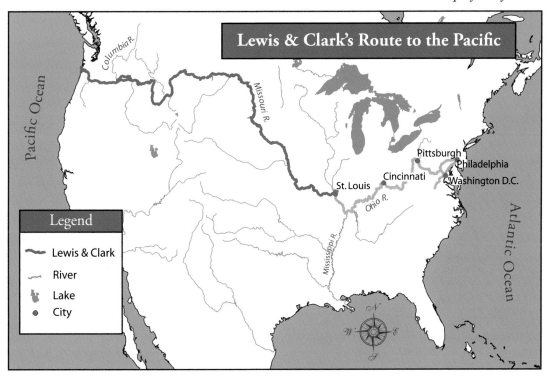

history revealed new perspectives on events near the end of the Corps' stay but also on the early days of the Corps' arrival at the Pacific.

While Lewis and Clark's journey west has been exhaustively researched, authors and historians mostly skimmed over what happened after the party arrived at the Lower Columbia River. That's what Rex Ziak, a cinematographer and lifelong area resident, found when he began researching the explorers' trek in the early 1990s.

Lewis and Clark historian Rex Ziak pauses during a talk titled "Fur Trade, Soft Gold, Lewis and Clark." Ziak uses passages from history books and a historic map of the United States to illustrate his talk. (Photo by Sandra Swain, The Daily Astorian.)

At first Ziak's only goal was to memorize the dates when Lewis and Clark arrived at (December 7, 1805) and departed from (March 23, 1806) Fort Clatsop. But as he studied further, he found few other details about what happened to the group after it first arrived at the river's mouth.

Most puzzling was the fact that it took the party just a month to travel more than 500 miles from Idaho to a campsite near Pillar Rock, on the Washington state shore, where Clark entered his famous journal note "Ocian in View!" on November 7th. But it was another entire month before the group reached the spot where they established their winter encampment at Fort Clatsop—a period that's ignored by most Lewis and Clark scholars.

Before Lewis and Clark engulfed his life, Ziak's passion was ancient Rome, and he marveled at the tiny details of this or that campaign that embroiled historians in lengthy debates as they dissected, word by word, every scrap of information about the period.

"I went back to those Roman scholars, how they found out where Julius Caesar decided to cross the Rhine River in 55 B.C.," he said. "I wondered if I could apply that analytical research to this."

Ziak began a meticulous reading of the explorers' journal entries, describing their struggle the last few miles downriver toward their goal. "You have to read it one line at a time," he cautions. Ziak noted any and all details about the weather. He contacted a meteorological specialist in Maryland who plotted the ocean tides for that period. He walked that stretch of the riverbank, hiking into the tiny coves and creek drainages where the explorers took refuge during the winter storms that pinned them to the north shore for days on end.

"It was a puzzle I started to piece together, little by little," he said.

What Ziak put together was a thrilling account of danger and despair, of a ragged, chilled, hungry group of explorers so close to their goal they could hear the ocean, but pinned down to the shore by wind and waves as the rising tide flooded their campsites.

"At Dismal Nitch on November 10th, there is just one point between them and the ocean—all they have to do is go around that point. But the conditions are so terrible they turn around and go back. On November 10th, the Lewis and Clark Expedition comes to a complete stop," he said. "This story here is arguably as historic and dramatic and grueling as any other segment of their expedition."

Heavy fog enclosed the expedition. Rain soaked the explorers. Outbursts of hail, thunder, and lightning halted their progress. Rocks tumbled down the steep hill into their camp. Clark described their predicament in his journal:

> It would be distressing to a feeling person to See our Situation at this time all wet and cold with our bedding &c. also wet, in a Cove Scercely large enough to Contain us . . . our party has been wet for 8 days and is truly disagreeable, their robes & leather Clothes are rotten from being Continually wet. [November 12, 1805]

The spot, dubbed "Dismal Nitch," is now commemorated in the Lewis and Clark National Historical Park on the present-day north side of the Columbia River near the Astoria Bridge.

Ziak also came to a conclusion about the next important point on the Corps' journey. He claimed that Station Camp, the tiny spot a mile west of the Astoria Bridge on the Washington shore that the group reached on November 15, 1805, was the true end of the Lewis and Clark Trail, the spot where Clark wrote "This I could plainly see would be the extent of our journey by water."

The sandy beach at Station Camp provided a much-needed respite. The explorers camped comfortably, constructing shelters from boards they took from the houses of what appeared to be an abandoned Chinook village. Station Camp served as Clark's primary survey station, and is the place where he took the most precise compass readings and produced the most detailed map made during the entire expedition.

Clatsop Indians reported that game was plentiful on the south side of the Columbia. The captains gave each member of the expedition a vote on whether to cross the river in search of elk or to backtrack upriver to build a winter camp. Sacagawea, their Shoshone guide, and York, Clark's slave, were given the privilege of voting on this matter at a time when women and African Americans did not have voting rights in the United States. Some historians have subsequently referred to Station Camp as "the Independence Hall of the West." The party voted to cross the Columbia in search of elk, although Sacagawea disagreed. Clark recorded her vote "in favour of a place where there is planty of Potas [wapato roots]" in his journals.

Ziak first explained his findings in a two-part essay published in *The Daily Astorian* in November 1997. His research eventually resulted in the book *In Full View*, his day-by-day account, complete with detailed descriptions of weather and tides, of the explorers' month-long adventure on the lower river. His claim didn't go down well with many on the south side of the river, he said, but it helped spark new interest in the saga and a cooperative effort between the two states to tell the full story of Lewis and Clark's arrival.

"Lewis and Clark did not see this as Oregon and Washington; they saw a river with two banks," he said.

Ziak's research also helped Station Camp and Dismal Nitch gain recognition in the Lewis and Clark National Historical Park. Ziak traveled to Washington, D.C., in 2006 to testify before a congressional committee in support of the new, expanded park.

"What I was trying to tell the senators in Washington was the immense significance of a place called Dismal Nitch and a place called Station Camp," he said. "It would have been a lot easier if they had been called Little Big Horn and Pearl Harbor."

THE LONG WINTER

Upon leaving Station Camp, the Corps began looking for a direct crossing of the open water between Station Camp and the south shore of the Columbia River—a risky expedition for the group's heavy canoes. The explorers backtracked upriver to a point where the Columbia was narrower and full of islands that made crossing easier.

After crossing to the south bank, the expedition again moved west, toward the river's mouth, to find suitable winter quarters—dry land, fresh water, timber that could easily be felled, and most importantly, an abundant supply of elk and deer.

The Corps of Discovery landed at a high point of land above the Netul River, the present-day Lewis and Clark River, on December 7, 1805. Their landing is marked in the Lewis and Clark National Historical Park by the Historic Canoe Landing and Netul Trail.

In the midst of the swampy, temperate rain forest, Lewis and Clark selected the rise above the river as the location for their winter camp.

In spite of all of the written accounts recorded by the expedition members, we know surprisingly little about the original construction of Fort Clatsop. Neither can we verify its precise location and description.

The first diagram of Fort Clatsop appears on the cover of Captain

William Clark's journal. It shows the location and dimensions of the various rooms, along with doors, gates, and fire pits. The drawing is labeled "50 foot Sq." As authoritative as Clark's diagram appears, the captain drew it before construction began, likely as a guide to the rest of the party, and then he left to blaze a trail to the ocean. But it is still the only visual record of the fort's original layout, and Clark, who was the faithful chronicler of the party's day-to-day activities, never mentioned in his journals if his design was or was not followed.

In 1899, this was declared the approximate site of Fort Clatsop. (Photo from the Oregon Historical Society Research Library, OrHi 1695.)

This view across Youngs Bay shows where Lewis and Clark wintered in 1805–1806. (Photo courtesy of Lewis and Clark National Historical Park, National Park Service.)

The men began cutting trees on December 10th. Captains Lewis and Clark moved into their new quarters just two weeks after the first trees were cut, and the remaining members of the party joined them on Christmas Day, when Clark noted "all the party Snugly fixed in their huts." Having shelter from the wet weather was most likely the greatest joy for the members of the Corps that day. The stores of tobacco and whiskey were exhausted, and there were no provisions for a holiday feast. Clark wrote:

> We would have Spent this day the nativity of Christ in feasting, had we any thing either to raise our Sperits or even gratify our appetites, our Diner concisted of pore Elk, so much Spoiled that we eate it thro' mear necessity, Some Spoiled pounded fish and a fiew roots.

In late December, after the fort had been completed, another group set out to establish a salt works. The Corps had exhausted its salt supply. Although Clark himself was indifferent to using salt to improve the taste of meat and fish, the rest of the party wanted it to help with the bad taste of their diet, which was predominantly rotting elk meat. Salt also helped preserve fresh game, which was necessary at Fort Clatsop because winter temperatures were not cold enough to keep stored meat from spoiling.

Constant rain most likely plagued the Corps' treks along the coast. The winter of 1805–1806 at Fort Clatsop was wet and miserable. During the 106 days spent at the fort, they counted 94 days of precipitation, including 17 days of snowfall, and only six days of sunshine.

The inclement weather almost certainly made staying dry and keeping warm the group's top priority. They treated various ailments and injuries, prepared for the journey home, and traded with the friendly and sophisticated traders, the Clatsop people. The expedition's priority was finding food. Every day a hunting party of several men journeyed out as far as 15 miles from the fort and spent several nights in the open. Along with meat, the hunters supplied skins that were tanned using animal brains and wood smoke. The party was constantly at work making clothing, including more than 300 pairs of moccasins. They also repaired equipment and rendered animal fat to make candles.

The captains were absorbed with re-writing their journals. Clark used his field drawings and measurements to produce astonishingly accurate maps. Some scholars feel that we would not have the expedition's detailed journals and maps without the winter spent at Fort Clatsop.

SHREWD TRADERS

Trading was probably not as easy at Fort Clatsop as it had been during other parts of the Corps' journey. At the dawn of the 19th century, ships from Europe and Boston were circumnavigating the globe to get to the Pacific Northwest, where a lucrative fur trade with Native American tribes had long flourished.

By the time Lewis and Clark completed their trek to the "ocian in view," they were not the first white people the Native Americans had encountered.

By the time the expedition got to present-day Clatsop and Pacific counties, the days of bargain-basement prices for furs were long gone. To test the waters, Rex Ziak said, Clark offered his watch and handkerchief and some coins for otter skins, but the Native American tribes he encountered refused to trade.

Ziak said Clark concluded that the local tribes had an unusual culture of sharp dealers—different from other tribes they had encountered.

Despite the savvy traders and miserable weather, the expedition made it through the winter in relative comfort. Lewis wrote that "Altho we have not fared sumptuously this winter and spring at Fort Clatsop, we have lived quite as comfortably as we had any reason to expect we should; and have accomplished every object which induced

This potato patch filled part of the fort site in 1899.
(Photo from the Oregon Historical Society Research Library, Neg 26294.)

our remaining at this place except that of meeting with the traders who visit the entrance of this river."

The original Fort Clatsop started to disappear almost immediately after the Corps of Discovery left it in 1806. Little is known about what happened to the fort in the years following Lewis and Clark's departure. Much of the site's nineteenth century history was composed from scant accounts from visitors and homesteaders.

On October 2, 1811, only five years after the Lewis and Clark Expedition departed, an employee of John Jacob Astor's Pacific Fur Company, based in the just-founded town of Astoria, reported that Fort Clatsop's remains "were but piles of rough, unhewn logs, overgrown with parasite creepers."

Two years later, a visitor to the site reported "willows 25 feet high" growing inside the fort. In the 1830s, another visitor said that "the logs of which (Fort Clatsop) is composed are still perfect, but the roof of bark has disappeared, and the whole vicinity is overgrown with thorn and wild current [sic] bushes." Carlos Shane, who lived at the site during the 1850s, described removing two remaining cabins to build his house in 1851: "In clearing away for my house I set fire to the remains of the old cabins and endeavored to burn them."

From 1887 through the early 1900s, half of the rights to the mineral and clay under most of the Fort Clatsop claim were owned by a variety of clay companies, including the Oregon Pottery Company, the Western Clay Manufacturing Company, and Gladding, McBean & Co. The exact length of time of each company's operations on the site is unknown.

In 1899, a representative of the Oregon Historical Society, Olin D. Wheeler (a writer for the Northern Pacific Railway), Silas Smith (grandson of Clatsop Chief Coboway, who had received the fort from Lewis and Clark upon their departure), four local residents, and a photographer established the approximate location of Fort Clatsop. Wheeler instigated the trip because he was planning to retrace the footsteps of Lewis and Clark. The local residents gave information that helped identify the site.

Although no surveyors accompanied the local residents when they estimated the site, the residents' claims must have been enough for the Oregon Historical Society. The society began purchasing the land, including clay rights, in 1901.

HOMESTEADER REMEMBERS LIFE AT THE DESERTED SITE

In 1957, 87-year-old Harlan Smith recorded details about his childhood at the Fort Clatsop site. Smith was only eight in 1880 when he and his parents left the site for Portland, but his memories provide a personal look into the era.

When Harlan Smith and his family moved to the Fort Clatsop site, they threw a housewarming party. All their neighbors, some living as far as six miles up the river, attended. Six miles was a long way in 1872—the "Lewis and Clark neighborhood," as Smith called his community, had no roads, and the people who lived there traveled by non-motorized boats.

Everyone at the party sang songs while Smith's mother played her organ. One of their neighbors brought a bass viol with him across the Great Plains, so it is likely he entertained the guests as well.

The house that Harlan Smith's grandfather built either burned or was salvaged by others for its wood. When Smith and his parents moved to the site in May 1872, they lived in a tent while they built a house. Smith recalled: "I remember my father hauling the lumber up on the baby cart and my mother protesting that he might break the baby cart. He hauled the lumber up from the landing to the site where we built our house."

For the first three or four years, the Smiths got their drinking water from a nearby spring they nicknamed "Iron Spring," after the iron deposit ringing it. Harlan Smith's father then dug a well and after that, Smith remembered, "we didn't use this

Mrs. and Mr. Harlan Smith at Fort Clatsop in 1955.
(Photo from the Clatsop County Historical Society.)

spring any more, except my sister fell in it one day when she was about three and I was about five, and I had to pull her out."

Harlan Smith's mother told him that one of the logs partially buried near their house was from the original Fort Clatsop:

"That is the Look-Out Tree. That is what my mother told me when we first went there—that is what Lewis and Clark had used for their lookout . . . These big knots—they left them about three feet along, all the way up from the ground, so a man could go out there and climb right up, like a ladder, on those long knots."

The Oregon Steam Navigation Company contracted with William Smith to build a road from Fort Clatsop to Clatsop Plains. Vacationers to the Oregon beaches had to travel a sandy and treeless road from their steamer dock to Seaside, Oregon. William Smith thought a shorter road from Fort Clatsop, through two miles of forest, would make for a more enjoyable trip. The company provided two shovels, two mattocks, and one or two axes, and paid two Chinese immigrants one dollar a day to help Smith, who donated his labor. The men completed the work in two or three months, using an old Native American trail and an elk trail as guides, for a total of $150 per mile. The road later became a county road and is now a segment of the park's Fort to Sea Trail.

Once the road was built, Harlan Smith and his family would drive a farm wagon to the shore "and splash in the ocean, which we thought was a great treat." The new road also meant more tourist steamers docked there.

Smith's sister "used to climb up in one of [the saplings on the property] when the men were cutting the saplings, and have them cut it and let her fall down in it—she liked the ride, falling right down in the trees." There were many alder trees on the property, and the Smiths hung a board from one, as a swing for Harlan Smith and his sister.

Before moving to the Fort Clatsop site, William Smith operated the Buena Vista Pottery Company. The land around the fort was rich with clay, so he opened a brickyard and sold the bricks in Astoria. When the Smiths moved to Portland in 1880, William Smith eventually started the Portland Pottery Company, and got his supply of clay from the Fort Clatsop site.

Information and quotes for this section were taken from a July 6, 1957, tape-recorded interview of Harlan C. Smith with archaeologist Paul Schumaker and historian John A. Hussey of the National Park Service, Region Four; the tape is stored in the history files of the National Park Service, Region Four, San Francisco, California.

Sergeant Nathaniel Pryor and George Drouillard (from left) admire 12-year-old Jordan White's gloves at Lewis and Clark National Historical Park during the Bicentennial Commemoration. Matt Hensley, portraying Pryor, and Jim Phillips, portraying Drouillard, are history re-enactors who trade with visitors like White, of Oregon City. (Photo by Lori Assa, The Daily Astorian.)

THE SHOW MUST GO ON

IN THE MIDST OF REBUILD, BICENTENNIAL PROCEEDS
Two centuries after the Corps of Discovery arrived at the Pacific, the setting around Fort Clatsop looked much as it did in early December of 1805. Two men who looked like Meriwether Lewis and William Clark erected tents, chopped firewood, stripped trees for tipi poles and traded with the "natives" for much-needed supplies. But this time the "natives" offered peculiar gifts.

"Captain Lewis, have you ever heard of yogurt?" one "native" asked. Captain Lewis admired another visitor's umbrella. "This is fascinating, I should have such a device," he said.

Yogurt and umbrellas weren't staples of the Clatsop tribe two centuries ago, but the re-enactors portraying members of the Corps of Discovery made a few concessions to 21st-century tastes during their stay at the park for "Destination: The Pacific," the Lewis and Clark Bicentennial Commemoration November 11–15, 2005. Chewing gum offered by another visitor was equally mysterious—Astoria school teacher Tom Wilson, portraying Sergeant John Ordway, asked what tree it came from, and after sampling some said it was completely unlike the pine pitch the men sometimes chewed, but agreed to make a trade for it anyway. The explorers would have been eager to trade, said Chip Jenkins, Superintendent of the Lewis and Clark National Historical Park. "It was the start of winter, they were living under rotting elk hides, they were short of food and supplies—put yourself in their moccasins," he said.

The first-person re-enactment program gave visitors the opportunity to talk one-on-one with re-enactors and to ask questions about the journey. The 20 re-enactors—the most the park had ever hosted—gave visitors to the Bicentennial a glimpse of what life would have been like in the first days of the Corps' arrival at the Fort Clatsop site.

The Living History program was just one small part of "Destination: The Pacific," five days of events at the Lewis and Clark National Historical Park. Event organizers had predicted that the park's commemoration would be one of the biggest of 15 signature events nationwide during the three-year Bicentennial. Since its kickoff in Virginia in early 2003, the Bicentennial has a drawn a core following of "Clarkies," or dedicated Corps of Discovery fans, who were expected to attend the events along with the local and regional guests.

Before the October 3rd fire, the fort was to be the setting for the first-person Living History program, and just hours after the fire, community members began pledging their labor and donations to build a new replica, some hoped in time for the Bicentennial.

The original Fort Clatsop was built in three weeks by men wielding simple hand tools—imagine what a motivated group of workers could do today, said many people eager to see the fort rebuilt. But the replica built in the 1950s by a volunteer-led effort took 18 months from the time it was first conceived to final completion.

Faced with cold, rainy weather, history re-enactors Michael Riley and Clinton Smith (from left) get a taste of what the Corps of Discovery experienced in 1805. The re-enactors were part of the Bicentennial Commemoration's Wintering Over program. (Photo by Lori Assa, The Daily Astorian.)

Chip Jenkins said rebuilding the fort wouldn't take anywhere near as long as that. But while he and the rest of the park staff had been overwhelmed by the public response to the fire and the offers of immediate help, he wanted the new Fort Clatsop to be as much a national treasure as the one it would replace, and that was going to take longer than six weeks. "Our goal is a legacy," he said.

Event organizers eased the community's fears by quickly altering the Living History program and other events planned for the fort. Their quick thinking paid off. The fort hosted about 3,500 people—twice the number the park saw during the same weekend in 2004.

"Nobody canceled as a result of the fire—in fact, people wanted to be a part of a new layer of history," said Cyndi Mudge, executive director of the "Destination: The Pacific" Bicentennial event.

Organizers mastered the art of improvisation during a weekend of events that started off with heavy rain and high winds, similar to the weather Lewis and Clark experienced during the winter of 1805–1806. At the November 11th opening ceremony at Fort Stevens State Park, regular squalls sent many of the estimated 2,000 onlookers scurrying for cover under tents, camera platforms, and even the fort's historic concrete bunkers.

"I think you're overdoing the atmosphere," Governor Ted Kulongoski joked as rain pelted the audience. The weather didn't stop the pageantry that wove historical, tribal, and military themes together in the Veterans Day event, which included music from a U.S. Army band, traditional Native American singers and drummers, and a procession of American Indian military veterans carrying the flags of their tribes along with an American flag.

The former fort was once the site of a Clatsop Indian village whose members traded with Lewis and Clark.

"It was in this area that Lewis and Clark met our people," Joe Scovell, chairman of the Clatsop-Nehalem Confederated Tribes, said. "It was a friendly meeting." Kulongoski, who appeared with Washington Governor Chris Gregoire, called the Bicentennial "one of the greatest moments in Oregon cultural history." The former Marine joined a procession of veterans—Native American and non-Native American—who circled the audience in a traditional Native American honor dance.

The weather was calmer Sunday morning for the Consider the Columbia event on the Astoria Bridge, but the stiff wind and fog that did appear were enough to scrub some elements of the program. The event featured about 500 people assembling on the bridge for a ceremonial pouring of waters from four rivers on the Lewis and Clark Trail—the Mississippi, Missouri, Snake, and Clearwater—into the Columbia in a symbolic joining of the five waterways.

Just east of the bridge, the charter fishing boat Shamrock carried a small group who watched as Robert Archibald, president of the National Council of the Lewis and Clark Bicentennial, and Allen Pinkham, Sr., of the Nez Perce tribe, emptied the water from the four rivers into the Columbia.

The Clatsop County Fairgrounds' Festival of the Pacific that featured music, food, and arts and crafts vendors was, for the most part, sparsely attended. The festival's Kids Corps of Discovery was the exception to the low attendance at the fairgrounds. Volunteers led more than 1,500 kids in hands-on activities such as Native American games, bead trading, and animal tracking lessons. Organizers attributed the low attendance at fairgrounds' activities to a lack of day-visitors from Portland because of the bad weather.

Attendance at the "Ocian in View" lectures, which included talks

by local historian Rex Ziak, Lewis and Clark scholar Gary Moulton, astronaut Bonnie Dunbar, and interpreters Hasan Davis and Amy Mossett, reached almost 100 percent, while about 1,000 people attended the "Merry to the Fiddle" concerts in Astoria.

Like the Corps of Discovery's journey, the Lewis and Clark National Historical Park and the Bicentennial events included sites throughout Oregon and Washington. The Corps of Discovery II traveling exhibit, which set up in Long Beach, Washington, on November 7th, featured educational displays, an outdoor encampment, and lectures in its "Tent of Many Voices." A total of 16,693 people visited the exhibit, a number believed to be the second-highest total at any national bicentennial signature event.

Early on, Bicentennial organizers were determined to cross state lines for the commemoration events, said Jan Mitchell, chairwoman of the planning committee for "Destination: The Pacific." That cooperative effort played a major role in the creation of the new park in 2004. Various local, state, and national dignitaries joined with hikers to dedicate one part of the park, the Fort to Sea Trail, on November 13th. They praised the collaborative community effort that completed the trail just in time for the Lewis and Clark Bicentennial.

"The trail is a lot better in reality than in my preconstruction imagination, so I think we have a lot to be proud of," said Oregon State Senator Betsy Johnson, chairwoman of Oregon's Bicentennial organizing committee. Mary Oberst, wife of Governor Ted Kulongoski, led an estimated 400 hikers on the new trail. The governor, who was

Corps of Discovery re-enactors brave the chilly weather at the Lewis and Clark National Historical Park-Fort Clatsop. (Photo by Lori Assa, The Daily Astorian.)

originally slated to attend the dedication, gave a send-off to the hikers before traveling to a memorial service.

"The (Bicentennial) commemoration will soon be part of our cultural history," Oberst said, reading from Kulongoski's prepared statement.

The project's final price tag of $3.3 million was financed through partnerships between state and federal agencies, private businesses, the Oregon National Guard, and nonprofit groups like the Northwest Youth Conservation Corps and the Student Conservation Association. David Evans and Associates, Inc., design firm lined up 13 businesses, including architects, engineers, and landscapers, who loaned their services to the project. The Conservation Fund purchased 900 acres along the trail route from Weyerhaeuser Corp., and held the land until the National Park Service could buy it.

"Everyone knows it wasn't the federal government that did this project—that's why it was done so well," said Kit Kimball, director of intergovernmental affairs for the Department of the Interior, who represented Interior Secretary Gale Norton at the trail dedication. "This was done by all of you—it was a grass-roots project, and hopefully we were there to help."

The dedication included a special Lewis and Clark song from a chorus of first-, second-, and third-graders from Astoria's St. Mary Star of the Sea Catholic School, and a speech from "Thomas Jefferson," portrayed by re-enactor Bill Barker before the group began the hike.

"To the sea, to the sea!" Chip Jenkins called, urging people down the final stretch of the trail.

The 6 ½ mile trail begins at Fort Clatsop and follows an old wagon road west to a lookout at the top of Clatsop Ridge, then winds down through thick forests to U.S. Highway 101 near Rilea Armed Forces Training Center, where an underpass carries hikers under the highway. The path skirts the edge of Camp Rilea and passes coastal wetlands to the trailhead and parking lot on Sunset Beach Road. From there it winds the last one-third mile to a viewing platform overlooking the ocean.

The trail is intended to roughly parallel the path that Lewis and Clark's group used to reach the beach from Fort Clatsop during their winter stay in 1805–1806.

Cindy Orlando, former superintendent of Fort Clatsop National Memorial, was among those in attendance. She said the event was an emotional occasion for her. Orlando led the park for nine years in the 1990s when the trail project was proposed, but was unable to push the project forward.

A 149-acre parcel at Sunset Beach owned by Clatsop County was a key piece of the project, but county commissioners were reluctant to turn over the land to the NPS as the original planning for the trail began in the 1990s. In early 2002, the commissioners came within one vote of selling the land for a golf course, but almost two years later the board, with two new members, sold the property to the Oregon State Department of Parks and Recreation for the Fort Clatsop trail project.

"We had a vision, and it's great to see it has been implemented," Orlando said. It took another month before the National Park Service purchased the land to secure the next park site, Dismal Nitch, a mile east of the north end of the Astoria Bridge on State Route 401.

Today riprap lines the gently sloping shore of the Dismal Nitch park site, but in 1805, the site was a dark tangle of trees and boulders where the Corps of Discovery took shelter from fierce storms that nearly halted the Corps' journey.

The storms pinned the group to the narrow shoreline for several days. "The most disagreeable time I have experienced," William Clark wrote in his journal. Lewis and Clark's party eventually took advantage of a lull in the weather to paddle around Point Elice and land at Station Camp, where they declared their westward journey completed.

Sean Johnson (left) and Payton "Bud" Clark walk with other Corps of Discovery re-enactors on the newly-dedicated Netul Trail. (Photo by Lori Assa, The Daily Astorian.)

Congress officially named the site Clark's Dismal Nitch in November of 2004, keeping Clark's misspelling of *niche*. The Corps' safe haven is currently marked by a rest area; but thanks to the Conservation Fund's December 2005 purchase of 154 acres of woodland surrounding the niche, the park will be expanded.

"The addition of Dismal Nitch is absolutely vital to ensuring preservation of this national treasure," said Washington Congressman Brian Baird.

In March of 2006, another piece of history was preserved with the dedication of the Netul Trail, which linked the park with the Netul Landing parking area. The landing pays homage to the spot where Lewis and Clark docked during their trip down the Netul River from Youngs Bay, which is directly to the north.

Netul Landing now serves as a way station for the Fort Clatsop shuttle bus, a canoe and kayak launch site, and a viewpoint for waterfowl and bald eagles. Interpretive panels at the site tell the story of the Corps of Discovery's stay at Fort Clatsop and portray the culture of the Native Americans who inhabited the Lower Columbia River at that time. A life-sized bronze statue of Sacagawea, the only woman on the expedition, completes the exhibit. From Netul Landing, the Netul Trail runs one and a half miles north to the Fort Clatsop replica, about six miles south of Astoria off Highway 101. The trail ends just a few hundred yards below the fort, where reproductions of the dugout canoes that transported the Corps of Discovery are docked.

Payton "Bud" Clark helped commemorate the new trail by offering a farewell to the hundreds of spectators on shore who watched as he and the rest of the his group of historical re-enactors, Discovery

Expedition of St. Charles, Missouri, paddled down the Lewis and Clark River on March 23, 2006. Clark's departure marked the end of the Bicentennial on the 200th anniversary of Lewis and Clark's departure.

The Discovery Expedition group led a hike on the mile-long pathway, which winds along the bank of the Lewis and Clark River.

When Lewis and Clark departed, they handed over Fort Clatsop to the local Clatsop Indians. On March 23rd, Clatsop-Nehalem Confederated Tribes leaders Joe Scovell, of Turner, and Diane Collier, of Warrenton, were presented with replicas of the original peace medals given to tribal chiefs along the trail, and reproductions of the letters that Lewis and Clark gave to the local tribe on the day they departed Fort Clatsop. Collier in turn gave traditional necklaces of beads and shells to some of the dignitaries.

Tom Wilson, one of the park's local re-enactors, spoke of the bonds that developed between Lewis and Clark's party and the local Native Americans, who traded with the explorers for food and other goods without which they most likely would not have survived. "That bond and friendship, 200 years ago, continues," he said. "Through thick and thin, this relationship has come full circle."

The dedication of the Netul Trail included a thank-you to the Port of Portland, which provided a timely $10,000 grant to acquire a land easement that allowed the project to go forward.

At the send-off at Netul Landing, there was more gift-giving, including tokens of appreciation to and from the Clatsop-Nehalems and Nez Perce. "Meriwether Lewis," a.k.a. Bryant Boswell from the Discovery Expedition, gave Clatsop-Nehalem members updated versions of Lewis and Clark's farewell letters that expressed the thanks of the group. The expanded park offers attractions like the new trails that many people have yet to discover, sites that will be treasured far into the future, Chip Jenkins said.

Clatsop County's role in the Bicentennial events officially ended with the dedication of the Netul Trail and the ceremonial departure of Lewis and Clark in March, but most of the events wrapped up in November 2005.

Despite the absence of a replica Fort Clatsop and the nuisance of inclement weather, the event was deemed a success. Along with drawing lasting attention to the park, the Bicentennial left behind a stronger bond between Oregon and Washington and a better sense that the two states share the Lewis and Clark story. The events also increased awareness about the Native American presence in the Lower

Corps of Discovery re-enactors journey from Netul Landing to Tongue Point in a Chinook canoe. (Photo by Lori Assa, The Daily Astorian.)

Columbia region, said Cyndi Mudge, executive director of the "Destination: The Pacific" Bicentennial event.

"The fact that our communities are more aware of the tribal nations out here, the Clatsop-Nehalem and the Chinook, is a lasting impact as well," she said.

"Destination: The Pacific" board members.
Front Row (Left to right): Cyndi Mudge, Executive Director of Lewis &
Clark Bicentennial Association (LCBA) & "Destination: The Pacific"
Planning Committee (DTP); Jan Mitchell, Chair of DTP Planning
Committee; Kitty Paino, LCBA Board member; and
Karen Myhr, LCBA Administrative Assistant.
Middle Row (Left to right): Major Alisha Hamel, Oregon National
Guard, ex officio LCBA Board & Chair of the DTP Opening Ceremony;
Diane Collier, LCBA Board member representing Clatsop-Nehalem
Confederated Tribes; Les McNary, President of LCBA and Chair of DTP
Committee for Festival of the Pacific; Jean Harrison, Chair of the DTP
Honors Reception; Una Boyle, DTP Committee member and Pacific
County Friends of Lewis & Clark (PCFLC) Board member; and
Carolyn Glenn, DTP Committee Chair for "Ocian in View" programs
and former president of Pacific County Friends of Lewis & Clark.
Back Row (Left to right): Chip Jenkins, Superintendent of Lewis & Clark
National Historical Park; Frank Little, LCBA Treasurer and Opening
Ceremony Committee member; Roger Rocka, Chair of Consider the
Columbia event; and Ed Cook, DTP Committee Chair
for Corps of Discovery II: 200 Years to the Future.
(Photo courtesy of the Lewis & Clark Bicentennial Association.)

The Ultimate Tribute

History doesn't record that Thomas Jefferson was waiting on shore to welcome Lewis and Clark at the final stop of their westward journey.

But on November 15, 2005, as hundreds of spectators watched, the third president of the United States—in the person of re-enactor Bill Barker—extended his hand to the explorers he had sent west as they stepped from their dugout canoes onto the

Retracing the journey of the Corps of Discovery, re-enactors row dugout canoes into Chinook County Park, Washington. (Photo by Lori Assa, The Daily Astorian.)

Columbia River shore. To accommodate life in the 21st century, "Destination: The Pacific" Lewis and Clark Bicentennial events were held November 11–15, 2005. Lewis and Clark didn't actually arrive in the area until November 15, 1805. The Bicentennial's date was changed to avoid clashes with Thanksgiving weekend plans, but members of the Discovery Expedition of St. Charles, Missouri honored the historic dates with ceremonies to mark the Corps of Discovery's movements around the region.

"Thomas Jefferson," portrayed by re-enactor Bill Barker, breaks character long enough to take a picture of the Discovery Expedition rowing in. (Photo by Lori Assa, The Daily Astorian.)

The all-volunteer St. Charles group retraced the entire Lewis and Clark Trail from Elizabeth, Pennsylvania, to the Pacific Ocean, camping overnight at or near the same campsites used by the explorers, as closely as possible to the 200th anniversary of each day's stop. They completed their 4,100-mile re-enactment of the Lewis and Clark journey by paddling to the shore of Chinook County Park at Chinook, Washington, on the same date

Lewis, portrayed by Bryant Boswell (left), and Clark, portrayed by Payton "Bud" Clark (center), prepare to consult members of the Corps of Discovery on where to spend the winter of 1805–1806. (Photo by Gary Henley, The Daily Astorian.)

that Lewis and Clark's party, after a week pinned to the north shore of the Columbia by fierce storms, managed to round Point Elice and reach the broad, sandy beach they dubbed "Station Camp." It was there the Corps of Discovery, "in full view of the ocian," declared their westward trek complete, and where the captains polled the members, including Sacagawea and York, on where to spend the winter.

At the November 15th event, "Jefferson" read out the complete instructions that were given to Lewis for his journey, and asked the captains—played by Bryant Boswell and Clark descendant Payton "Bud" Clark—about their discoveries.

"Lewis" told the president that the "perspective from Monticello" of a symmetrical continent with an easy portage over a modest continental divide was mistaken, and that there was no fabled Northwest Passage. The event wrapped up with an exchange of gifts between Clark and Ray Gardner, vice chairman of the Chinook Nation Tribal Council, who helped paddle a replica native canoe alongside the St. Charles re-enactors.

"I thank the Chinook for welcoming us into their homeland," said Clark, after presenting Gardner with a replica of the Jefferson peace medal that the original Corps of Discovery gave to the Native American tribes it encountered. Gardner in turn gave Clark and Boswell each a bead necklace.

Gardner said after the ceremony that he hoped the attention the Bicentennial brought to the region would help the tribe's effort to regain federal recognition. To begin with, members of the St. Charles group will share the Chinooks' story when they return to their home states, he said.

After a decades-long effort, the tribe was granted recognition in early 2001, but that ruling was reversed a year later following an appeal by the Quinault tribe.

"One of the things the government used against us (in denying recognition) was that they said the local community did not know we exist," he said. "The more we are out in public, the more we let people know our story, they will not be able to use that argument."

The group also took part in the November 24th re-enactment of "the vote" at Station Camp when the expedition members, including Sacagawea and York, were polled on where to spend the winter. Re-enactors commemorated the Corps' arrival in Fort Clatsop by paddling their way in dugout canoes to the boat landing at Netul Landing just south of the park, completing the final leg of their ambitious re-enactment of the explorers' westward journey. On shore to greet the group were members of the Clatsop-Nehalem Confederated Tribe, who offered the re-enactors salmon, oysters, and other traditional native foods.

"Thanks for making it so special by joining us," said Payton "Bud" Clark of Dearborn, Michigan, the great-great-great-grandson of Captain William Clark who portrayed his ancestor. "It's a special day for us, and it's bittersweet, the end of our journey that we began in January 2003, when we had the honor of firing a volley over Monticello."

Jeff Reynolds plays the violin for Sacagawea, portrayed by Jan Falcon, and her "baby," Jean Baptiste, during the re-enactment of the vote on where the expedition will spend the winter. (Photo by Gary Henley, The Daily Astorian.)

The St. Charles group, however, will remain active through the rest of the Lewis and Clark Bicentennial and beyond, Boswell said.

"There's no doubt we'll do portions of it, if not all of it. We have so much invested in it," Boswell said. The group returned to Oregon in March 2006 to re-enact Lewis and Clark's departure from Fort Clatsop. But even after the end of the Bicentennial, members of the group—including five descendants of the Lewis and Clark expedition—still want to continue sharing the Lewis and Clark saga, particularly with children, Boswell said. "We've seen the benefits of bringing history alive to young people," he said.

Ray Gardner (far left), vice chairman of the Chinook Nation tribal council, explains that a canoe becomes a respected part of a tribe during a canoe blessing and dedication ceremony in Long Beach, Washington. (Photo by Lori Assa, The Daily Astorian.)

National Park Service and Oregon Department of Forestry staff clean up after the fire.
(Photo courtesy of Lewis and Clark National Historical Park, National Park Service.)

Rebuilding an Icon

NEW REPLICA RISES FROM THE ASHES

Many emotions were running through Fort Clatsop Park Superintendent Chip Jenkins as he watched, sometimes in tears, as firefighters doused the flames on the smoldering ruins of Fort Clatsop late on the night of October 3, 2005.

But one of the strongest was determination.

"I knew we would be here—I knew we would rebuild the fort," he said as the new Fort Clatsop replica was dedicated on December 9, 2006. "I didn't know how or how long it would take. But by 10 o'clock the next morning, it was obvious we were going to follow the example of 1955."

Just hours after news of the fire first broke, the community immediately stepped forward in a big way. Citizens handed checks to park employees to help fund the fort's reconstruction, and everyone from "reasonable craftsmen" to the Oregon National Guard offered their help. The Astoria-Warrenton Area Chamber of Commerce held an emergency meeting two days after the fire and pledged its support to the rebuilding project. Longview Fibre, Hampton Affiliates, Stimson Lumber, and Weyerhaeuser Corp. immediately offered to donate logs for the project. Interior Secretary Gale Norton directed the National Park Service to make all necessary resources available to the park, and Governor Ted Kulongoski visited to offer the state's assistance.

Building the original Fort Clatsop took three weeks. The 1955 replica was built with volunteer labor in 18 months. Many had hopes that modern technology would allow the new replica to be constructed quickly, possibly before the Bicentennial just six weeks away. But a hurried rebuild would have robbed the park and the community of two rare opportunities.

From the very beginning, Jenkins and the park staff wanted the community to be just as fully involved in every stage of the project as it was in 1955. The park staff also wanted to examine recent historical research into the structure and conduct further archeological studies around the fort site.

"The fort built in the 1950s was very successful because it really connected people to the story," Jenkins said. "Our goal was to be that successful."

GETTING TO WORK

Even with the outpouring of community support, rebuilding the fort took planning and a lot of hard work.

That work started with the clean-up and demolition of the site. Sixteen Oregon National Guard soldiers, all volunteers for the job, joined personnel from the National Park Service and Oregon Department of Forestry to take apart and remove the charred ruins. The crew worked carefully, and largely by hand, for a number of reasons. Access to the fort site through the surrounding forest was limited and park staff did not want to clear space for large machinery. According to Jill Harding, the park's chief of visitor services, care also was taken not to disturb the site below ground level.

The workers had to take precautions against the chemicals, such as arsenic, that were used to treat the logs in the 50-year-old structure. They wore gloves and breathing masks as protection. The wood posed no hazards to the fort's many visitors over the years, but the fire likely released some of the toxins, making the charred logs potentially harmful.

Logs, planks, and cinders that were shoveled into plastic garbage cans were hauled by ATVs and a small tractor to dumpsters provided free by Western Oregon Waste. The debris was taken to a special waste site in Hillsboro. Virtually every piece of wood in the structure was touched by the fire; the only pieces not burned to some degree were the two gates on either side of the parade ground.

With the debris cleared, the archaeologists dug in. They hoped to find artifacts under the fort that might give some sign of the history of the site (see sidebar: "The Curse of Fort Clatsop").

Meanwhile, a design team assembled by the Lewis and Clark National Historical Park was busy coming up with a blueprint for the new fort. The design effort attempted to balance historic authenticity with modern concerns for safety and durability, while creating an icon as enduring as the original replica.

Rebuild project coordinator Pete Field said the designers used the plans of the first replica as a starting point, then they combed through the Lewis and Clark journals, eyewitness accounts from fort visitors after the explorers' departure, and more recent scholarly research for information on the fort's likely appearance. They also took some clues from the program "The Big Build" on the History Channel, which had featured an episode where a group in Kansas built a Fort Clatsop replica using 200-year-old tools and techniques.

The team determined that, like the first replica, the new one would be based on Clark's famous journal diagram of the original Fort Clatsop—showing the location and dimensions of the various rooms along with doors, gates, and fire pits, and labeled "50 foot Sq." But the decision wasn't without controversy.

DISCREPANCIES IN THE JOURNALS

As authoritative as Clark's drawing appears, the captain actually drew it before construction began, likely as a guide to the rest of the party, before he left to blaze a trail to the ocean. But later journal entries written by various Corps of Discovery members raised some questions about the building's actual layout.

Private Joseph Whitehouse described the layout of the Corps of Discovery's encampment as "three lines composed 3 squares, & the other square we intend picketing in, & to have 2 Gates at the two Corners."

Along with Whitehouse's description of three lines and squares, Sergeant John Ordway writes in his own journal about the group beginning "the last line of our huts forming three (sides of a) Square . . . the other Square we intend to picket and have gates at the two corners, So as to have it a defensive fort."

In a journal entry for March 23, 1806, the day the party departed, Whitehouse described the fort as "an oblong Square, & the front of it facing the River, was picketed in, & had a Gate on the North & one on the South side of it."

From those few clues, some have deduced that Fort Clatsop may have been a U-shaped structure, with three lines of rooms, or "huts" as the party called them, with a picket stockade enclosing the fourth side. Staff at the Lewis and Clark National Historical Park admitted the original fort very well could have been U-shaped, but said they found too few concrete clues about the fort's actual shape to warrant such a major change in its design.

"The journals are very detailed about some things, but there is remarkably little said about what the fort looked like," Jenkins said.

Clark, who was a faithful chronicler of the party's day-to-day activities, never mentions in his journals that his design was not followed, according to Pete Field, the project manager for the fort rebuild.

"Building this original layout has some very good logic," Field said. "We need to fall back on a defensible decision."

But that hardly meant the case was closed on Fort Clatsop's actual design, and the park planned to offer visitors a chance for intellectual exploration by highlighting the uncertainties about the original Fort Clatsop. Jenkins envisioned an exhibit that would show all the relevant journal entries about the fort's design, and then allow visitors to create their own fort, perhaps with Lincoln Logs, based on what they believe the journals show.

"Read everything—what do you think it might have looked like?" he said. "We want to highlight that there are discrepancies within the journals."

The park staff helped spark scholarly research into the journals by working with National Park Service historians to evaluate the available information about what the fort might have looked like, an area that has been mostly overlooked by Lewis and Clark historians,

Jenkins said. The park also made a commitment to publish information and encourage additional peer-reviewed academic research.

NPS Historian Frederick L. Brown published a detailed examination of the journals in the Winter 2006 issue of the *Oregon Historical Quarterly*. The article, titled "Imagining Fort Clatsop," points out that the journals of soldiers working on the fort indicate the possibility of a three-sided structure, but Brown writes that the evidence is not conclusive.

If more evidence about the fort's design comes to light, the park will be open to changing the replica, Jenkins said, noting that the first replica was modified numerous times as new information about the original fort arose.

"If over the next five or ten years a consensus emerges that the fort was a different configuration, I believe the National Park Service would work to make those changes," he said.

DESIGN CHANGES

While the new Fort Clatsop was built on the old replica's footprint—even using the original concrete footings, with the same number of rooms and the same roofline—there were a number of changes.

For starters, the 1955 replica used 50-foot logs on the outer walls, but the design team decided to use logs between ten and twenty feet long.

About 420 logs were donated by area timber companies for the project. These totaled about 17,000 board feet, enough to build three homes.

"We just wanted to help restore the fort," said Curt Copenhagen from Longview Fibre, which donated logs along with Hampton Affiliates, Stimson Lumber, and Weyerhaeuser Corp.

Longview Fibre's logs came from company tree farms in Clatsop and Columbia counties, including one south of Elsie. The company supplied wood to a number of log-home builders, who used logs the same dimension as those requested for Fort Clatsop, Copenhagen said. Still, the design team had some particular specifications for length, diameter, and taper, so the company harvested trees picked specifically for the replica.

The specifications for the logs were drawn up by Laurin Huffman, a historical architect with years of experience overseeing modifications at Fort Clatsop. Huffman was one of the principal designers of the new fort.

To determine what size of logs the Corps of Discovery likely used to build the original fort, Huffman considered what types of loads the builders would have been capable of moving around on their own, and concluded that the eight- to ten-inch-diameter logs to be used in the replica were probably as big as a group of ten to fifteen people could have handled.

Of the 33 people in the expedition, several had left with Captain Clark to find a route to the sea, and others would have been out hunting, leaving no more than a dozen or so of the members available to construct the fort. That would limit the size of the logs the party would have used.

"A common misperception of Lewis and Clark is that they would go after this old-growth cedar," Huffman said, noting that it was unknown whether the explorers even had any saws available for the task. "You just can't handle an old-growth cedar log."

This misconception also assumes that there were many old-growth trees around at the time. Some researchers have found evidence that the coast's forests may have contained many young stands of trees at the time of Lewis and Clark's arrival, the result of an earthquake and tsunami believed to have struck the Northwest coast in 1700 and large forest fires that followed, Jenkins said.

While many think the Corps of Discovery didn't even bother to peel the bark off the logs used in the original fort, the logs for the new replica were peeled, mostly because that was the only way they could be pressure treated, Pete Field said.

"Remember, their fort only had to last three months—we want this one to last 50 or more years," Field said. Peeling logs also provided an interesting opportunity for community involvement.

PITCHING IN

Just two months after the fire, hundreds of volunteers, from local residents to Boy Scouts to National Guard troops, gathered at Clatsop County Fairgrounds to peel logs for the new fort.

Rosemary Johnson, a Fort Clatsop volunteer whose husband, Curt, and son, Sean, were interpreters at the park, was among the volunteers. Johnson said it was her first attempt at peeling logs, but that it only took a few hours to get the hang of it. Like many other volunteers, she said she wanted to lend her labor because the project gave her a connection to the new fort.

"I can tell my grandkids I had a part in it," she said.

AJ Hudgik was one of a group of Oregon State University College of Forestry students who volunteered for the project. A recreation major, Hudgik was especially excited to be working on such a prominent project as Fort Clatsop, which she visited as a child. "And I'll still be around to see it in 50 years," she said.

John Markham of Arch Cape carefully used a drawknife as he

John Markham of Arch Cape uses a drawknife to strip bark off a log. Markham was one of more than 100 volunteers, many from out of state, who came to the Clatsop County Fairgrounds to de-bark logs for the new Fort Clatsop. (Photo by Tom Bennett, The Daily Astorian.)

stripped a log down to the wood. "This seemed like an opportunity to leave part of myself on the fort," he said.

Dick Jones of Nehalem said he donated money to the rebuild project, but decided to get actively involved, too. "Even an old man can peel logs," he joked.

"It's too bad (the fire) happened, but it's great to see all the people come out to help," Jones said. "That's what's great about the North Coast—people do help, all you need to do is put the word out."

Members of Boy Scout Troop 100 from Albany also answered the call. Troop Leader Dan McMinds heard about the project from his son at Oregon State University, and brought a half-dozen scouts, ages 11 to 16, to Astoria. Members of the troops had been working on a number of projects toward earning a special Lewis and Clark badge, he said.

Workers used only shovels, draw knives, axes, and other simple hand-tools to strip the logs down to the raw wood—the logs had to be completely bare for treatment. Modern mechanical debarkers could have done the job much more easily, but a more labor-intensive approach was exactly what organizers wanted, according to Pete Field.

"Most importantly, the community really wanted to be involved in the rebuild . . . so this was the easiest, safest way to get the most people involved," he said.

Using rough tools also gives the logs a textured, hand-hewn look, something the designers were aiming for to make the new replica look more historically accurate than the 1955 structure.

"You couldn't really get that with the other (debarking) processes,"

Field said. "So we'll get a look that on a real micro scale will look real authentic—if Lewis and Clark had de-barked the logs."

It was long accepted that the first replica was probably much more expertly crafted than the one Lewis and Clark's wet, tired men threw together in a few weeks in December 1805.

Carl Fabiani carefully marks the location of a cut in a log for the Fort Clatsop replica at the Clatsop County Fairgrounds. (Photo by Tom Bennett, The Daily Astorian.)

Tom Ables guides a log into place on the captains' quarters side of the Fort Clatsop replica. (Photo by Tom Bennett, The Daily Astorian.)

"We've been consistently hearing if we could make it look more rustic," Jenkins said while planning the new replica.

Jenkins said the community debarking would help create that rough look but that it was "more about connecting kids and families and people to history, having people here to help make history, more than it was about reproduction."

Along with log peeling, volunteers helped construct the new fort; split planks for the fort's roof and floor; hauled logs; and constructed bunks, tables, and benches. By the time the new Fort Clatsop replica was dedicated in December 2006, about 700 people had participated in the project.

"If it were not for the volunteers, all we would have would be a building. With the volunteers, we have a project of the heart," Jenkins said.

After enough logs were peeled, National Park Service builders from Mount Rainier National Park in Washington brought their woodworking skills to the task of recreating Lewis and Clark's 1805 winter encampment at the Clatsop County Fairgrounds. It is the responsibility of the Mount Rainier workers to repair and maintain the park's two hundred historic structures. But the Fort Clatsop project offered special challenges, said team leader John Carney.

"I've done other log work projects, but never from the ground up," he said. The main challenge in building Fort Clatsop was making something that would last and still look rustic.

While the builders were hoping to re-create some of the original fort's rough-cut look by using an axe to rough up chainsaw cuts, they decided the axe-cut would allow water into the joints, speeding decay. Instead, the cuts were smoother and resulted in a cleaner join. To add to the rustic appearance, the ends were cut to chopped-off points instead of the neatly sawed ends of the 1955 replica.

Another builder, Barry McMonagle of Bellingham, Washington, also builds log and frame homes on his own. Logs, with their round shape and uneven dimensions, are much tougher to work with than standard lumber, he said.

"The common assumption is that if it's rustic, it's easy to do, but it's the opposite, he said.

After the fort was assembled, workers took apart and numbered the logs so they could be reassembled in exactly the same order at the park after they had been treated at a facility in Hillsboro, Oregon.

FORT CLATSOP RISES AGAIN

The first logs were put in place at Fort Clatsop on February 22, 2006. Park staff, National Guard members, interns from the Student Conservation Association, and citizen volunteers helped carry logs from the park's parking lot to the fort site, where woodworkers from the Mount Rainier National Park began the task of reassembling the pieces.

Lance Koach was one of the several volunteers who joined the project. He left his home in Vancouver, Washington, at 4:00 a.m. so he could be part of history and "something I can point out to my kids," he said.

"It makes you wonder how (Lewis and Clark's men) did it without even the equipment we have," he said.

Enlisting volunteers to help manually carry the logs was not only part of the park's effort to engage the public in the process, but also a way to minimize the use of heavy equipment in the project, said

Jenkins. A temporary trail leading directly from the parking lot to the fort site was put in to make the log-hauling easier.

"When we're done, we don't want it to look like a construction site," Jenkins said.

The logs were sorted out in the parking lot so they could be carried into the construction site where workers from Mount Rainier

Volunteers carry a log into the Fort Clatsop site. (Photo by Lori Assa, The Daily Astorian.)

carefully lined up the first logs—any misalignments in the first stage of construction would only get worse as the walls got higher.

"These are not like Lincoln Logs—they're not all the same size," Jenkins said. "They're all custom-made—if we break or damage one, we'd have a problem."

With the aid of an excavator, Mike Anderson from Mount Rainier National Park carefully guides a log into place in the captains' quarters side of Fort Clatsop. (Photo by Lori Assa, The Daily Astorian.)

After the logs were carried in, volunteers helped apply a paste-like substance called Tim-bor—the second stage of the preservation process that was recommended to the park by Jeff Morrell, a self-described "professor of wood rot" from the Oregon State University College of Forestry, Jenkins said.

The logs of the first replica were "wolmanized," or injected with a preservative solution in a pressurized chamber. The solution included a number of toxic chemicals long since banned in wood treatment. While the logs of the new fort were also pressure-treated, the new preservative, while safer, wasn't quite as effective. So, to complement the pressure-treating, the Tim-bor, a nontoxic insect- and fungus-fighting compound, was poured into grooves cut into the logs.

A metal fastening was used to anchor the logs at the top of the structure, but otherwise the fort was held together by the weight of the logs.

"Part of the reason we're not putting any steel into it is we're looking down the road in case they need to replace individual logs," said John Carney.

Despite intermittent rainfall and heavy labor, volunteers who helped carry the 300-pound logs were cheerful and excited to be participating in history.

Linda Tozer of Tigard said she and her husband have been "Lewis and Clarking" for the past five years since hearing a lecture by historian Rex Ziak of Naselle, Washington. The couple came out to help peel logs at the fairgrounds and were back to pitch in.

"We want to be part of making sure history is preserved," she said.

The crew members assembling the new Fort Clatsop put the

last log in place on March 10, 2006, and then, a few days later, cut out some of the doorways and installed a picket gate at one end of the fort.

The fort replica was still roofless and floorless and missing doors, chimneys, and pretty much every other amenity, but it was standing, just five months after the fire. And it was constructed in time for the March 23rd event, "The Return Home," a commemoration of Lewis and Clark's departure from Fort Clatsop in 1806.

Some major items, such as the roof and doors, were not installed until later in order to give the logs the chance to dry and settle. The logs, which were harvested specifically for the Fort Clatsop project, weren't dried before construction, and would have shrunk, according to Laurin Huffman.

The walls would contract by a quarter-inch or more per foot, which could have cause havoc if the roof and doors had been installed in March, Huffman said. Builders also waited to place the chinking and daubing in the gaps between the logs.

"We'll let the wind blow through it for a while," Huffman said.

When the new structure was designed, no vertical dimensions were specified, just a set number of logs. Since the logs are different diameters, the real height wasn't known until the fort was actually built.

"The logs work out to what the logs work out to," Huffman said.

Just how much the logs could shrink was clear to John Carney. He left a ladder leaning against one of the walls, and three days later when he went to retrieve it, the settling logs had wedged it tightly against the ground.

The logs, then a rich, golden color, would likely darken and turn slightly gray as they dried, Huffman said.

"It would be nice if we could keep it looking fresh and new" just like Lewis and Clark's fort likely looked in its brief period of use, he said.

The logs of the original replica turned a shade of green over the years, something that was first attributed to the chemical treatment process, Huffman said. It was later found that algae were giving the fort its greenish hue.

"It will probably end up green again," he said.

Because the fort had already been assembled once at the fairgrounds, the work at the park was relatively simple. The Mount Rainier crew's main challenge was to ensure that the bottom logs were exactly in position on the foundation before building up the walls—one inch off on the 50-foot length could have thrown off the entire project.

After the logs were allowed to dry, shrink, and settle, the roof, doors, floors, and other fixtures were installed in time for the December 9th dedication, about the same time Lewis and Clark's crew began constructing the first Fort Clatsop 201 years before.

While the structure was essentially completed in December 2006, there were still a few details to be finished. The rustic design called for leaving gaps between the log walls, much like in the original Fort Clatsop. Instead of the mud, twigs, and moss Lewis and Clark's men would have used to seal up the walls, the park staff would likely use a synthetic material for more durability, according to Ron Tyson, the park's chief of maintenance.

At the time of the dedication, a fireplace had been built only in the captains' quarters; the park completed the fire pits in the other rooms in February 2007. They were designed to minimize the risk of another accidental fire, Tyson said.

Just as important as the new fireplace design, however, was the comprehensive training that all park staff would receive on fire safety, said Tyson. From now on, staff will have to become certified before they are able to build fires in the rooms' fireplaces.

The fort includes a new detection system that picks up any high temperatures and triggers an alarm. A sprinkler system was originally proposed but ultimately not included, in large part because of the low water pressure at the park. Tyson said the park had requested funding to build a bigger water line that would make a fire-suppression system more feasible.

The alarm system alone will go a long way toward ensuring that any fire draws a quick response, said architect Laurin Huffman. Because the fire crews did not have an exact location when they were alerted to the fire in October 2005, crews drove around the area in search of the blaze before locating it.

Building a new fort from scratch also allowed for some other improvements, such as a fully handicapped-accessible doorway into the orderly room, which allows people in wheelchairs and electric scooters to come into that room and the adjacent captains' quarters.

At the dedication ceremony, Chip Jenkins spoke to a crowd of more than 400 people who had come to celebrate the fort's completion. Along with the local residents who built the original replica in 1955, Jenkins thanked the park's own staff, the Oregon National Guard, the Mount Rainier National Park woodworking team, National Park Service archaeologists, architect Laurin Huffman and Project Coordinator Pete Field, and the local fire departments who responded to the fire. He also thanked Oregon's congressional delegation, who

An emotional Chip Jenkins, the superintendent of the Lewis and Clark National Historical Park, speaks at the dedication ceremony for the new fort replica. (Photo by Lori Assa, The Daily Astorian.)

within hours of the fire were contacting the Secretary of the Interior for support in rebuilding the fort.

Jenkins estimated the total cost of the new fort project would have been about $700,000 if the National Park Service had funded the work through a standard government contract. But with the outpouring of support and donations, for everything from volunteer labor to the logs and tools, the actual cost was much lower, Jenkins said. Costs not covered by donations were paid for out of the National Park Service's emergency appropriations budget, he said.

Speakers at the dedication ceremony, including Oregon State Senator Betsy Johnson, a spokesman for U.S. Senator Gordon Smith, and Steve Shane, the vice chair of Clatsop-Nehalem Confederated Tribes, praised the community effort that went into the new fort's creation.

Senator Johnson recalled the "anguished" phone call she received from Jenkins at 3:30 in the morning following the fire, and the "profound sadness that fell on all of us" upon the news of the fort's destruction. But with the determined response of the park, the local community, and others, "tragedy turned into triumph," she said.

"This new replica galvanizes our collective relationship to this special place," she said.

The Curse of Fort Clatsop

The archaeological dig in search of signs of Lewis and Clark's winter encampment once again revealed some tantalizing signs in the soil that on further investigation turned out to be false leads.

Doug Wilson, an archaeologist from Fort Vancouver National Historical Site who led the exploration underneath the location of the first Fort Clatsop replica, explained that when researchers wrapped up several weeks of digging under Fort Clatsop, they had uncovered a handful of artifacts but no definitive signs of the explorers' famous winter home.

"The search is not really about what kind of evidence you find, but the process of discovery," Wilson said.

The fire that destroyed the 50-year-old replica on October 3, 2005, offered researchers the first opportunity in a half-century to take a comprehensive look under the structure. The group excavated under the replica's concrete footings in search of artifacts and subtle signs in the soil that might point to postholes or other signs of the original fort. Work began in the weeks following the fire and continued through November—even during the Bicentennial commemoration. The dig gave Bicentennial visitors the opportunity to watch the work and speak with the archaeologists as they searched the site.

The Fort Clatsop site has been notoriously stingy in offering up anything conclusively linked to the Corps of Discovery and its three-month stay, going back to early explorations of the site in the late 1940s and 1950s beginning with Louis Caywood, the first site archaeologist, Wilson said.

Caywood uncovered what he described as fire pits and whittled sticks that he said were likely evidence of the Corps of Discovery—the bored explorers probably spent the winter sitting around the fire whittling sticks, he surmised. Paul Schumaker, who dug an extensive network of trenches around the replica fort in the 1950s, found more fire pits and sticks that he also linked to the explorers.

But the mystery of the whittled sticks was soon solved by a lumberman who said they were buckhorns, the ends of tree branches found inside a tree's trunk.

It was the first time Fort Clatsop had fooled an archaeologist, but not the last, Wilson said.

In the 1990s researchers returned with more modern equipment, including ground-penetrating radar. Artifacts including trade beads and musket balls that may have come from Lewis and Clark's era were uncovered.

Also found were the remains of what appeared to be a human-dug pit. The researchers guessed it might be one of the fort's privies, and analyzed the soil for the high levels of phosphorous and mercury left behind in human waste. Unfortunately those tests showed no such concentrations, Wilson said.

The mystery of the privy, as well as Caywood's and Schumaker's fire pits, was solved when a small tree near the fort was blown over. The resulting hole in the ground was similar in shape to some of the "pits" uncovered in those earlier digs, and the archaeologists concluded that most of the holes that previous studies linked to Lewis and Clark were in fact the result of natural processes such as blown-down trees and burned stumps, Wilson said.

But when the archaeologists returned to the fort in 2005, they were hopeful they might finally uncover proof of the fort, he said. Most of the group had worked on the recent dig at Station Camp, where signs of a Chinook Indian village had been uncovered, and they were confident they could read the subtle shadings in the soil that pointed to human activity.

The "curse," however, was still working, Wilson said. Excavations found what appeared to be pits and trenches with unusually straight edges.

"We thought, 'this has got to be human-made,'" he said.

But further examination revealed that tree roots had left behind those pits and trenches. "We were skunked again," he said.

The artifacts uncovered ranged from a Native American stone tool to beer bottles. Some pieces that probably came from the homesteads that occupied the area in second half of the nineteenth century were also found.

"This puts the Lewis and Clark Expedition in context," Wilson said. "Lewis and Clark did not come into a vacuum, and they did not leave a vacuum."